Blood and Knavery

Sundrye ſtrange and inhumaine Murthers,
lately committed.

The firſt of a Father that hired a man to kill three of his children neere
to Aſhford in Kent:

The ſecond of maſter Page of Plymoth, murthered by the conſent of his
owne wife : with the ſtrange diſcouerie of ſundrie other murthers.
Wherein is deſcribed the odiouſneſſe of murther,
with the vengeance which God inflicteth on murtherers.

Printed at London by Thomas Scarlet.   1 5 9 1.

Blood and Knavery

A Collection of English Renaissance Pamphlets and Ballads of Crime and Sin

Joseph H. Marshburn
and
Alan R. Velie

Rutherford • *Madison* • *Teaneck*
Fairleigh Dickinson University Press

828.07

© 1973 by Associated University Presses, Inc.

Associated University Presses, Inc.
Cranbury, New Jersey 08512

Library of Congress Cataloging in Publication Data

Marshburn, Joseph H   comp.
   Blood and knavery.

   1. English literature—Early modern (to 1700).
2. Crime in literature. 3. Street literature—England.
I. Velie, Alan R., 1937–   joint comp.   II. Title.
PR1127.M3 1973   828′.07   72-3523
ISBN 0-8386-1010-2

Also by Joseph H. Marshburn:
Murder and Witchcraft in England, 1550–1640

Also by Alan R. Velie:
Shakespeare's Repentance Plays: The Search for an
Adequate Form

Printed in the United States of America

To our wives,
Mary and Sue

1.ɔ

Contents

Preface 9

Introduction 11

The Most Cruel and Bloody Murder 19

The Crying Murther 40

The Murder of Page of Plymouth 58

Murder upon Murder 65

Witchcraft 74

The James Hind Pamphlets 103

The Ranters Ranting 142

News from the Tower Hill 152

Look on Me London 159

A Treatise against Painting 176

A Short Treatise against Stage Plays 194

Preface

The scene is a hanging in late sixteenth-century England—a huge public spectacle. The rich and fashionable watch from splendid carriages, wealthy burghers sit on wooden bleachers erected for the occasion, and the hoi polloi climb nearby walls and trees or press around the foot of the scaffold. Hawkers abound, some peddling fruit, some pies, and some ballads and pamphlets describing the heinous crimes committed by the man being hanged. The ballads were short verse accounts of the sinner's transgressions, set to a popular tune. Pamphlets were longer prose accounts that were able to go into far more gory detail.

This book is a collection of English Renaissance pamphlets and ballads, some about capital crimes like murder, witchcraft, and highway robbery, others about less serious activities—though many thought them sinful—like using cosmetics and going to the theater. The purpose of the collection is to give the reader a glimpse into the lives and interests of the people of Renaissance England. It is intended for the general reader who finds the life of different historical periods interesting, as well as for the student who specializes in Renaissance literature and history.

The Renaissance was a period of rebirth and awakening in Europe, a period in which modern science was born, the New World was discovered and settled, and the arts flourished as never before. It was a fascinating age, a time that gave birth in England to Drake, Raleigh, Bacon, Shakespeare, and Milton. Virtually

9

everyone today is familiar with these titans. But in order to understand an age, it is important to know more than the titans; it is necessary also to know something of the common men of the time and the tenor of the daily life of the period—the stock from which the titans emerged and the background against which they flourished.

In his study of middle-class culture in Elizabethan England, Louis Wright raises the question, "Why study the man in the street, dead these three hundred years?" He answers,

> We must remember . . . that the Elizabethan tradesman, the average citizen, was the backbone of progressive enterprise in England and the direct ancestor of a civilization soon to predominate on both sides of the Atlantic. His vigor and strength enabled England to take its place in the front of nations.[1]

We attempt to cast some light on the Elizabethan man in the street by showing what he wrote and what he read—the popular literature of the time, which consisted primarily of pamphlets and ballads. The popular writers fall considerably short of Milton and Bacon in prose style, but little—if at all—in interest.

The Renaissance English were a highly literate people and, evidently, voracious readers. Publishers of the day poured out reams of matter to feed that hunger. We have culled what we feel are the most interesting of the ballads and pamphlets for this collection, emphasizing those which deal with activities that the Elizabethans felt to be criminal or sinful, because these activities elicited the most vivid writing. We believe that the collection will provide both the casual reader and the professional student with a valuable aid to understanding English life in the sixteenth and seventeenth centuries.

---

1. *Middle-Class Culture in Elizabethan England* (Ithaca, N. Y., 1958), p. 1.

Introduction

The term *popular literature* refers to the pamphlets and ballads written by professional writers and published by commercial presses for sale to the large English reading public. The term is used in contradistinction to the works of writers like Wyatt or Sidney who wrote for a select audience, and who took pride in the fact that they wrote for purposes of artistic expression, not to make money.

In 1500 few Englishmen could read, and those who could read little more than their Bible. However, by the time that Elizabeth took the throne in 1558, the production and sale of popular literature had become a thriving industry. In the century that followed the accession of Elizabeth, "The habit of reading became so widespread that by the outbreak of the Puritan revolution, the printing press was perhaps the most powerful single medium of influencing public opinion."[1]

Three factors account chiefly for the rise of popular literature: the introduction of printing, the spread of education and literacy, and the rise of the middle class.

The first English printer, William Caxton, set up shop in 1476 at Westminster, in the shadow of the Court and Parliament. At that time the outlook for publishing in England seemed bleak. The nation was still torn by the civil strife of the War of the Roses. Not only did few people have the leisure to read—the poor

---

1. Wright, *Middle-Class Culture,* p. 81.

worked from dark till dark, and the gentry were out fighting with the Yorks or the Lancasters—few were able to. For one thing, English was relatively new as a language of the educated classes. From the time of the Norman Conquest until the late fourteenth century, French had been the official language of England. The everyday speech of the aristocracy was French as late as the reign of Edward III (d. 1377). All subjects in school were taught in French until 1385.[2]

In addition, the Church controlled education and made literacy a possession of the few rather than of the many. The big breakthrough in literacy came with the Reformation. When the monasteries were dissolved in 1537, the Crown took over the task of education and offered learning to far more people than the Church had. Between 1540 and 1570 the Tudors established 139 schools, almost twice as many as had existed before. By the beginning of the seventeenth century, most Englishmen could read.

The new educational opportunities and extended literacy immediately affected the printing industry. In 1557, when the Stationers' Company was incorporated, ninety-seven establishments were accorded the privilege of printing and selling books.[3] The population of London being roughly ninety thousand at the time, this is an impressive figure,[4] and it increased throughout the sixteenth and seventeenth centuries.

The rise of the pamphlet and the ballad is linked to the rise of the middle class. During the sixteenth and early seventeenth centuries, the old feudal class structure and subsistence economy was replaced by the new order of capitalism. The merchant classes in the cities became wealthier and more powerful while the rural upper classes declined in fortune.[5] As the middle classes acquired

2. See G. M. Trevelyan, *History of England* (New York: Anchor, 1953), 1:309.
3. Wright, *Middle-Class Culture*, p. 82.
4. The "Directory of Publishers" in the 1969 edition of *Books in Print* lists approximately 1200 publishers in New York City—roughly one tenth as many proportionately as London had.
5. See L. C. Knights, *Drama and Society in the Age of Jonson* (New York: Norton, 1968), chaps. 1–3.

wealth, leisure, and literacy, they became a vast literary market for
the newly proliferating printers. Since there were no newspapers
or magazines, there was a great gap to be filled in light reading
matter, particularly of a topical nature. The ballad and pamphlet
filled this need.

The ballad—a short, rhymed narrative, generally set to a popular tune—was the first of the forms of popular literature to
achieve widespread circulation. From the inception of printing
until the early 1580s, the ballad was the principal medium
through which news reached the reading public. Ballads celebrated—or mourned—all the extraordinary events of sixteenth-
century life: wars, religious controversies, illicit love affairs,
witch trials, robberies, and murders.

Commercial publishers borrowed the printed format of the
ballad from the royal proclamation. The Crown had used proclamation sheets since the early thirteenth century to inform the
public about matters of importance. Printing greatly facilitated
distribution of proclamations. Printed proclamations used twelve-
by-nine-inch folio sheets. Since they were posted on walls, they
were printed on one side only, on what was known as a broad-
sheet or broadside.

The ballad aped the broadside format of the proclamation.
Publishers took topics of current interest, had them set in the
familiar ballad verse form, illustrated them with one or two crude
woodcuts, and issued them as broadsides on the folio sheet.

In the early 1580s the pamphlet replaced the ballad as the
most common form of popular literature, because its longer, more
detailed prose accounts gave a superior record of events.

The term *pamphlet* was generally understood to describe a
short, unbound work in either prose or verse (although prose
was far more common), designed to be sold to the public at min-
imum cost. Pamphlets were distinguished from broadside ballads
and books not by subject or medium, but by length and the way
they were bound. Ballads were one folio sheet; pamphlets usually

ran anywhere from eight to one hundred quarto or octavo pages. Books were longer than pamphlets, and were held together by a hard protective covering. Publishers produced the pamphlets by folding the folio sheet once to give four quarto pages, or twice to give eight octavo pages. Several of these units might be sewn together. The sheets were printed on both sides, and were stitched together by means of a bodkin.

Pamphlets were usually narrative in nature, and their range of subject was even broader than that of the ballad. In addition to the range of topical subjects—wars, crimes, and untoward phenomena like two-headed calves—there were sermons, plays, novelettes, and romances.

With popular literature came a new class of professional writers. Many were university graduates who lacked independent means of support. Formerly, many artists had been supported by aristocratic patrons, but as capitalism came to England, the aristocracy, whose wealth was based on land, declined in fortune. By the end of the sixteenth century most nobles found that supporting artists was a luxury they could no longer afford.[6] Many writers turned to pamphleteering as a means of earning a living. Around 1600, forty shillings was the going rate that publishers paid for a pamphlet in manuscript. Since at that time a skilled workman made at most a shilling a day, it is apparent that a writer who could sell the publishers at least one pamphlet a month could live comfortably by middle-class standards. The pamphleteers, however, thought that they deserved a good deal better, as is obvious from their frequent laments. One amusing statement of the pamphleteer's discontent is Ingenioso's tirade in *The Returne from Parnassus,* a satirical review put on at Cambridge in the opening years of the seventeenth century: "40 Shillings? a fit reward for one of your reumatick poets, that beslavers all the paper

---

6. *Ibid.,* pp. 112–16; and Alfred Harbage, *Shakespeare and the Rival Traditions* (New York, 1952), p. 97.

he comes by, and furnishes the Chaundlers with wast papers to wrap candles in: but as for me, I'le be paid deare euen for the dreggs of my wit. . . . "[7]

Part of the pamphleteer's objection was the ignominy that the university graduate felt in negotiating with a bourgeois publisher. Another sore point was that although there was money in pamphleteering, there was no prestige in it. There was a strongly ingrained idea during the Renaissance that it was shameful for writers to sell their work.[8] So, despite the fact that many of the better writers of the day tried their hand at writing pamphlets, contemporary critics looked with disdain on it. In discussing contemporary poets in 1586, William Webbe dismissed ballad makers and pamphleteers contemptuously: "If I let passe the vncountable rabble of ryming Ballet makers and compylers of sencelesse sonets, who be most busy to stuffe euery stall full of grosse deuises and vnlearned pamphlets, I trust I shall with the best sort be held excused."[9]

Balladeers were generally less talented and more obscure than the pamphleteers. Ballads were always published anonymously, and their authors are familiar only to a few scholars today. Louis Wright states:

> The broadside ballad was a form that unlearned men could soon acquire the trick of writing, and through it common folk found a means of self-expression. Certain citizen-writers like Thomas Deloney, William Elderton, Martin Parker, and Lawrence Price show the effort of poets of the people to supply what their public wanted and to express the ideas and ideals of that public.[10]

One important function of the balladeers was digesting and passing on culture to the masses much in the way birds swallow and regurgitate food for their young. The *pot-poets,* as they were con-

7. W. D. Macray, ed., *Parnassus: Three Elizabethan Comedies* (Oxford, 1886), p. 89.
8. Knights, *Drama and Society,* p. 86.
9. Wright, *Middle-Class Culture,* p. 92.
10. *Ibid.,* p. 420.

temptuously called, ransacked the world's literature for topics for their verse. Everything was grist for their mill: fiction and non-fiction, romance and history, current events and legend, even stories from the Scriptures were put into ballad meter and issued as broadsides.

In our collection we have concentrated on ballads and pamphlets dealing with sin and crime, since they are invariably the most interesting. Tales of two-headed calves have a certain curiosity value, and sermons may be uplifting, but they seldom called up the passion or vivid writing that the writers lavished on events that outraged them.

The authors take this occasion to make mention of the prompt and courteous cooperation of the following libraries: in England, at London, the British Museum, Lambeth Palace, Society of Antiquaries, the Public Record Office; at Oxford, the Bodleian; at Cambridge, Magdalene College; and Faversham Town Hall, where the Wardmote Book is housed; in the United States, the Huntington, the Folger, the Congressional; and here at Norman, the William Bennett Bizzell Library, University of Oklahoma. Finally, we should be remiss not to recognize the assistance of the chairman of our department, Dr. Victor Elconin.

Note: Throughout the anthology we have modernized spelling and standardized it. (Elizabethans often spelled a word or name two or three different ways in the same passage.) Punctuation has generally been left in its original state, save for occasional cases in which minor changes have been made to clarify the meaning.

Blood and Knavery

The Most Cruel and Bloody Murder

No act mesmerizes and appalls man like murder. Since the time of Cain, men have reacted with horror, outrage, and morbid fascination to the outrageous act in which one man dares to take the life of another.

In virtually every civilization, murder has been a favorite literary subject. It has inspired great works like the *Oresteia*, *Hamlet*, *Macbeth*, *Crime and Punishment*, and *Light in August*, as well as the popular sort of whodunit of Ellery Queen and Agatha Christie.

And, murder has always been newsworthy. In our time it is still the staple of the daily papers. In Elizabethan times it was the most popular subject of the pamphleteers and ballad makers.

Our first piece is "The Most Cruel and Bloody Murder Committed by an Innkeeper's Wife, Called Annis Dell." It is primarily the story of Elizabeth James, a girl of eight, who watches the murder of her parents and brother, and then has her tongue cut out to keep her from identifying the murderers. When she suddenly regains her speech some years later, her testimony leads to the conviction of her brother's murderers.

The story of the tongueless child who suddenly regains her speech is a remarkable dramatization of Hamlet's metaphorical statement of a Renaissance truism:

> For murder, though it have no tongue, will speak
> With most miraculous organ.

Most Elizabethan readers would simply have believed that Elizabeth's recovery was miraculous—an act of God. This was the point of view of our anonymous author. Modern readers are more likely to demand a scientific explanation. Anthony Boucher, in his introduction to a slightly

19

different version of the story, speculates that the child had been taught the "tollibon trick"—rolling up the tongue to play dumb—and that she used it to beg until the trauma of seeing the place of her brother's murder jarred her sufficiently to make her stop her pretense.[1]

This seems little more credible than the miracle theory. Elizabeth seemed very eager to help the authorities when they questioned her before she regained her speech, and communicating solely by gestures must have been very frustrating for her. Although the author specifically tells us that the tongue was cut out by the roots and thrown into the pond, it is possible that the glossotomy, done in haste with crude instruments, was not that thorough. Perhaps enough of the tongue was left to make speech possible, if garbled, and it was psychological rather than physiological damage that made the girl mute. In that case, perhaps the shock of returning to the place of her mutilation was therapeutic.

Whatever the real explanation, the important thing for us to realize is that the Elizabethans would have accepted the story with no questions. The idea that God took a direct hand in the daily operation of the universe, and that He suspended natural laws at will, was still prevalent. For Elizabethans, the moral of this story would have been the same as that of Chaucer's "Prioress's Tale" of the boy who continued to sing after his throat was cut: "Mordre wol out"—by divine agency, if necessary.

One detail that is likely to appall a modern reader as much as the murders themselves is the callousness of the Elizabethans toward a mutilated orphan. Master Allen, "pitying the misfortune of the child," cures her wound, but then sends her back out on the streets to beg for her living. It is not until the justices and knights of the shire find that she is the orphan of a substantial burgher that they give the town an "especial charge to provide more carefully for her, and not to suffer her any longer to lie in the streets."

---

1. Richard Barker, *The Fatal Caress* (New York, 1947), p. viii.

THE
MOST CRVELL
AND BLOODY MVR-
ther committed by an Inkeepers
Wife, called Annis Dell, *and*
her *Sonne* George Dell,

Foure yeeres fince.

On the bodie of a Childe, called
Anthony Iames in Bifhops Hatfield in
the Countie of Hartford, and now moft miraculoufly
reuealed by the Sifter of the faid *Anthony,* who at the
time of the murther had her tongue cut out, and
foure yeeres remayned dumme and fpeechleffe,
and now perfectly fpeaketh, reuea-
ling the Murther, hauing
no tongue to be feen.

With the feuerall VVitch-crafts,
and moft damnable practifes of one *Iohane Harrifon*
and her Daughter vpon feuerall perfons, men
and women at Royfton, *who were all execu-*
ted at Hartford *the 4 of August*
laft paft. 1606.

LONDON.
Printed for *William Firebrand* and *Iohn Wright,*
and are to be fold at Chrifts Church
dore. 1606.

THE MOST CRUEL AND BLOODY MURDER COMMITTED BY AN INNKEEPER'S WIFE, CALLED ANNIS DELL, AND HER SON GEORGE DELL, FOUR YEARS SINCE

Herodotus writes of Sesostris, a king of the Egyptians, of being carried in a chariot drawn with four kings, whom he before had conquered, when one of the four, casting his eyes behind him, looked often upon the wheels of the chariot; which Sesostris, earnestly noting, at last demanded of him what he meant by looking back so often, who replied, "I see that those things which were highest in the wheels become lowest, and the lowest as soon become highest, I think upon the inconstancy of things." Sesostris hereupon, as in a glass beholding himself, waxed more mild, and delivered the imprisoned kings from that slavery.

This history then, so lively expressing the mortality of man's life, that to the highest belongs a grave, as soon as to the lowest, and that man himself is a witness to himself, how uncertain are his days (since sin has spread itself like a leprosy over all flesh, and iniquity has gotten the upper hand), that a spider is able to choke us, a hair to stifle us, and a tile falling on our heads to extinguish us, and in that moment when we least suspect so sudden calamities.

Our life then is so momentary, that in that minute we breathe, if not defended by our Maker, in that minute we are breathless: Would any flesh, endowed with that heavenly reason which God has only given to man and angels, so forget his uncertainty, as for a little gold which is but the dregs of the earth, for vanity (the pleasures of the world) or for the world itself, which is a hypocrite, because it has exterior appearance of goodness, and within is full of corruption and vanity, which is but like to reeds, that when they shoot out first in the spring of the year, do with their fresh green color delight the eye for a while, but if we break them and look within them, we find nothing but emptiness and

hollowness, forget his Maker and the dignity of his creation, who made him like to Himself, to His own image and likeness, to the intent, that as all other creatures of their own proper natures do love their like, so should man set his affection on God alone, where contrarily, he being the hand of heaven, made for virtuous dispositions, conduct himself to vicious actions, whereby it follows certainly that men in their lives are like children, who more delight of a horse made of reeds, and babes formed of clouts,[1] than in the things themselves, so man gives more honor to the shadow than to the truth, and indeed (as in this whole course) but like birds, who greedily fly to peck up the corn till they be caught in the gin;[2] or like fishes, who earnestly swim to catch the bait, though they be choked with the hook; so do many, how indirectly soever, hunt after riches, till they deface their bodies be[3] the law, and condemn their souls by their sin, as shall appear by this following discourse.

Some four years since near Devonshey Hundred in Essex lived a yeoman, one Anthony James, who in repute of the world was counted rich, and by the report of his neighbors held credible and honest.

This man in the desire of his youth matched himself to an honest country maid, whose virtuous disposition equaled his own thoughts, and whose diligent care was carefully to save what her husband brought home, as his labor did strive to procure it abroad; so that the providence of the one and the care of the other mixed such a mutual content between them, that they lived like Abraham and Sara, he loving to her, she obedient to him.

In process of time this couple, growing wealthy by their labor, proved to be as happy by their issue, for it pleased God to enrich them with two children, a boy and a girl, that the wishes of the

---

1. Cloths.
2. Trap.
3. By? Evidently a printer's error.

father might be as well satisfied as the desire of the mother, and both contented in so comfortable a blessing.

The mother being (as women use to say) stored first with a daughter, and called it by her own name Elizabeth James, so that when time brought the father as happy rejoicing of a son, he christened it by his own name, Anthony James. In the education and bringing up of these two children, there was a pretty loving contention between the goodman and the wife, which of the two should prove most happy to the parents' delight, whose love indeed was alike to them both. So that time passing away in that comfortable strife between this loving couple, the daughter had attained to the age of eight years, and the son to seven, in which passage the mother having no other issue, was then with child with the third, and the better half of her time had carried so happy a burden.

About that season of the year a fair happened in Essex, to which the servants they then kept, some for pleasure, the rest about necessary business, were sent, so that the honest yeoman with his wife and children were only left at home, when mischief like a bramble that takes hold on whatsoever it touches, caught this occasion, and wrought in the minds of nine, I cannot call them men, but villains, and another not a woman, but a beast, to make prey of these harmless four, and their increased possessions: but as—

Finis est primum in intentione
Ultimum in executione.[4]

So these wretches having fastened on this monstrous intent, made haste to the execution thereof, and so soon had attained to this wealthy yeoman's house, where finding little or no resistance, they first bound the man and the woman, and giving the two children to two of their associates to hold, the rest fell to ransack,

---

4. Loosely, "The end follows the beginning."

where not contenting themselves with that store of riches they found, as gold, silver, plate, rings, and other wealth, having made up their pack, they consulted with themselves for their further security, to make spoil of the owners. It was not long in question ere this hellish jury had given up as damnable a verdict, for (suspicion always haunting a guilty mind) they determined with themselves they could not be safe from pursuit, from attachment, nay from shameful death, which they worthily deserved, without the slaughter of the father and the mother, which they presently resolved upon, and then two of them stepping to the man, where he lay bound upon the ground, with their daggers stabbed him in the body, who, ere his speech left him, lifting up his eyes, begged only this of them, "Take my riches, I cared for them to bring up my posterity, but now they are yours, I give them you freely; then pity my wife, be merciful to my children." These his last words seemed to beget some remorse (seldom seen) in the men which were murderers, which the more than monstrous woman perceiving (as in a rage thereat) stepped to his wife, and calling to him with these words, "Talkest thou of pity," quoth she, "if thy eyes have yet left so much sight to be witness how I'll be pitiful? Behold how I'll perform thy petition." So drawing out her knife (an act too terrible to report, but the most damnable that ever was heard of, executed by a woman), she ripped her up the belly, making herself a tragical midwife, or truly a murderess, that brought an abortive babe to the world, and murdered the mother.

The good woman having not leave to cry, and her husband having not the use of speech, they both lift up their hands, rolled their eyes one to another, and with that said, but silent, "Farewell ever."

This tragical spectacle enforced all the rest, partakers in the robbery and actors in the murder, to remorse, nay even to a repentance; that done, this horrible action had a beginning: but sin always seeking securely to shroud itself in, they began now to question of their safety, and (as villains are ever one afraid and in distrust of another) they conclude now to share their purchase, and every knave to shift for himself.

Some urged, "Let us first kill the children, as we have done their parents"; others and the greater part glutted with the present object, and even ashamed of themselves and their sinful actions, not only denied, but confidently resolved they would be no further guilty in the blood of innocents. In brief they agreed every party to have an equal portion of this ill-purchased booty, which soon shared among them, and as it appeared, having more than they could tell what to do withall, they gave the remain to three of their consorts, of which the woman was one, to convey away the children from thence, and bestow them in what place soever, while they would give their parents burial.

This was as soon done as talked of; seven of them carried the dead couple from the house to a wood near adjoining, and there buried them, and the other three are gone to travel with the children.

These monsters thus divided, whether of a determinate before of ancient acquaintance, or drawn by what means soever, it yet rests undiscovered to the world. These two men, this woman, and these two children the next day, some three hours before night, came to Bishops Hatfield in Hartfordshire, seventeen miles from London, the children being on a horse in a pair of panniers,[5] the woman riding between them, as it had been to visit some of their friends, then they took up their inn at one Dell's house: and being brought to their chamber, they called for their hostess, when after some other parle[6] had between them, they demanded of her if she would be secret in a business they would unfold unto her, who presently without further pause, replied, aye, as God should judge her, would she, when straight they began to discover to her their whole proceedings, showed her what riches they had got, and told

5. Large baskets.
6. Conversation.

her they were willing to make her a partaker therein, only they craved her advice, how they should dispose of the children. All this was spoken in the hearing of the girl. To which Dell's wife, as by the sequel appeared soon gave this her consent and instruction, that the boy should be murdered, and his sister have her tongue cut out.

This thus resolved upon, they fell to drinking, and who so merry as this devilish company; all this while the girl sat on the frame at the table's end, and in the meantime, the boy was strayed down the stairs, where being playing up and down in a lower room, this Dell's wife, having a laborer at work in her backside[7] to make her bavins,[8] called Nicholas Deacon, it was his chance to come in to call for drink, where taking note of him, by the prettiness of the behavior he used; his hostess passing by him, demanded of her whose child he was, who answered he belongs to a guest or two that are now above, the honest laborer having drunk his drink that he came for, went back to end his business in the yard, while the child (they being above in the heat of their cups, and not regarding him) strayed out into the street, where one Henry Whilpley, the tailor, taking notice of him, especially by a green coat with nine skirts about the waist, the fashion then being new for children, he called the boy to him to take a pattern thereof, and having satisfied his desire by noting it well and taking measure of the child, the tailor as the laborer, goes back to his work, and the boy returns to Dell's house.

By this time night coming on, as the fit mark for villains to act their villainies under; these wretches having supped with the children, as if no such pretense, which inwardly they intended, had lurked in their bosoms outwardly, bare themselves fair to the little ones and when they thought it fit time, went to bed together all in our chamber, the chamber having three beds in it, the men together, and the women with the children, who in the dead of

---

7. Backyard.
8. Bundles of wood.

the night, the time created for quiet rest, the ease of labor, and the honest man's repose, these homicides rising from their beds, and having a candle ready, awakened the children, made them ready, and with flattering words told them, they must go to their father and mother, when they poor hearts (as willing to obey, as they to demand, little dreading they were going to such a shambles,[9] as they had prepared for them) came down with them, and at the stairs' foot stood the son to this hostess called George Dell (who belike the mother had acquainted herein) and calling to the men bade them come on and doubt nothing, for he had seen the coast was clear, whereupon opening the back door, they went into the yard, where this innkeeper's wife used to milk her kine, and in which stood a great stack of wood, where delivering the girl to the woman and George Dell to stay with, took the boy, leading him behind the pile, first stopping his mouth with cow dung that he might make no noise, they slit up his throat from one ear to another. This inhuman murder thus acted, they returned to the house, told Dell's wife and her son the deed was done: quoth Dell's wife, "Then George, thou shalt conduct them to Bottomless Pond, where for our more safety, they shall end our cause of mistrust, or fear to be discovered by throwing him in." Then presently George Dell stepping to the woodstack, and choosing out a good big stake, he with the help of the rest bound thereon the dead child with a hair rope, and George Dell himself taking a long pike gaff on his shoulder, led them the way towards Bottomless Pond, being a mile from Hatfield, while the two thieves upon the stake carried the boy, and the strumpet led the girl in her hand. George Dell thus afore leading the way, the two thieves in the midst with the dead boy, after them comes (I may rightly call her so) the whore with the sister in her hand, who (what with drowsiness, and what with fear) seeing to lag, for the night being uncomfortable to men, it must needs be to children, the monstrous female (for

9. Slaughterhouse.

no woman) began to egg her on with fair persuasion, "Come apace sweetheart, thy brother is before, and we are going to thy father and thy mother."

The poor girl, encouraged with the remembrance of her parents' names, whose lives they had extinguished from her, as if the names of them (who first gave her life) could have created a new motion in her (as far as her childhood and feeble strength would give her leave), hastened after, and by the way called to her with these words: "Gammer, shall my mother make me ready tomorrow morning, kiss me when I come from school, and hear me say my lesson?" The devilish Devil answered (not having remorse, being remembered of the execrable act she had done), "Aye, when she sees thee next, she shall do all this."

The men hastening on before with the pitiful burden of a murdered brother, when she the divellisht[10] of all came after with a tender sister, and by the way began to ask her of several circumstances as where she was born, who were her parents, and what her name was; when the child answering to every question according to her remembrance so prettily, that if her leader had had left in her any spark of womanhood, who by nature are kind, flexible, and remorseable, and not been made up for one to be damned, she would have pitied her.

But who are created to be murderers, are created to be remorseless, and so was she, only beguiled the way with these and other such like questions, as what she walked upon, what she saw withall, and what she spake withall, when the innocent child (suspectless that her own tongue should be her own betrayer) according to her discretion answered to every one, directly pointing to her foot, her eye, and to her tongue, that with those, and by the help of those she saw, went and spake. Whereupon this bloody tigress, to make herself more monstrous, bade her put out her tongue that she might feel it (being at this time come just to

10. Most devilish.

a stile, where she sat down, and told the girl that they would rest themselves a while), when the child (little dreading it should be the last time she should make use of it, doing what she bade her), she presently caught it by the end, and with her thumbs wresting open the child's jaws to the widest she could stretch them, she cut it out by the root: the girl hereat beginning to make her just lamentation, this she-wolf holding her knife to her throat, bade her peace, or she would slit that as she had slit her tongue; so that for her pain enforced by fear (only as the blood exceeded in her mouth she still spat out that) the woeful child was quiet, when the strumpet bade her hold up her apron, and she would give her her tongue again, and "Look" (quoth she) "you lose it not, for you must bear it to your brother." By this time (with their conductor George Dell) the men had discharged themselves of their burden by Bottomless Pond, throwing the stake and boy they brought (and bound him withall) into a corn field, and the child with her tongue in her apron, and in the whore's hand had overtaken them, when presently went to act this last stratagem which before they had agreed upon, and threw the boy (as he was in his clothes) into the pond, giving him for his requiem fare-well, no other funeral rites and Christian burial, but these words, "Sink there instead of a mother-grave," the dead child thus in the pond, the whore (as if she had felt herself sick) not being an ex-ercised actor in more villainy, having forced the child to be sad (beholding first of her brother's untimely murder, and now of his watery grave) not resting here, made the distressed infant take her tongue (the instrument of her speech) out of her apron, and throw it after her brother, and as it was thrown from her hand, she uttered these words, "Let it go and spare not, it cannot be better bestowed, thy are near akin together."

The murdered brother thus bestowed, and his sister speechless, these villains having contented Dell's wife for her counsel, and so bountifully that where it was credibly known, the lease of her inn was (at the time of this action) at pawn for £250, she presently fetched it home, and bestowed a one hundred marks more in building. The next morning before day they parted; yet in their parting this was resolved upon between them, that the dumb girl with some little piece of money should be given unto a beggar to travel with, she so disposed of, they were certain never to be discovered.

The next day in Hatfield Wood (some two miles from Hatfield) this determination took effect, and a beggar for a piece of money took the wench, promising to keep her, as many such rogues use for one to beg withall. The child received, and the money paid, the two thieves and the whore departed: when the beggar (whether not liking the bargain lest after he should pay too dear for it, of slight care or self-will, it is yet unknown) he lost the child in Hatfield Wood, where shortly after it was found in a hollow tree, and having received some little cherishing of some well-disposed people about the woodside, from thence it strayed to Barnet, from Barnet to London, where happening in the dumb manner, it used to get at one Master Allen's door, a barber-surgeon, for some relief, the Master coming himself to the door, and seeing the child make such pitiful signs to the mouth, he took it by the hand and led it into his shop, and opening her mouth to know the cause of the grief it complained of, found the tongue to be cut out, and the wound unhealed, who (pitying the misfortune of the child) of his own charitable disposition, cured it. The mouth thus healed, for four years' space together, the girl hath been known in many countries to beg for her food, sometimes about London, sometimes in Essex, but most she hath been remembered (as is certainly by divine providence of heaven, that by her these villainies should come to light) to be resident in Hartfordshire, she was never known to speak any syllables tending to speech, only hoarsely she could mutter when anyone spake to her instead of answer, "Moka, moka," so near her tongue was cut out to the root, that the food any charitable persons bestowed on her, she had no tongue to help her to swallow it, but after she had chewed it in her mouth, she was fain to pull out the skin of her throat with her fingers, and gulp it down; in this dumb manner she continued four years. We will leave her begging for her living, and return to her murdered brother in Bottomless Pond.

This child having remained three weeks in the pond, on Saint Peter's Day in the morning (for at that time of the year happened this tragedy) some gentlemen and others (being a hunting for wild fowl) happened with their dogs to beat about this pond; when one of these dogs having scented the child (as where it was rose up under the weeds at a bankside) whined and cried, and by no means could be beat or drawn from thence, which eagerness of the spaniels wrought a desire in the men to know certainly the cause thereof, and with their long staves turning up the weeds, found there a boy to be drowned, as they considered; when carrying news thereof to the town, the body was by the crowner[11] taken up, and laid openly for the view of all men to take knowledge of it.

The whole country near thereabouts coming at the strangeness of the report, that a child should be murdered and then thrown into a pond, yet none could challenge in him the right of a son; yet the aforesaid Henry Whilpley, Nicholas Deacon, and divers others of Hatfield, made testification both by apparel and other signs (for the boy had a red head) that this was the child who three weeks before was seen in Dell's house, so many then signified to the justice: Dell's wife was sent for, for her husband was a blind man, when being demanded if such a child were not brought to her house (as before spoken), who they were that brought it thither, when she constantly denied, she knew of no such, and for certain she could affirm that no such child did lodge at her house, and being offered her oath, hereupon she was as

_____
11. Coroner.

ready to swear as resolute to deny, but who knows not lying and swearing are partners, and as inseparable companions as a thief and a receiver, and (as I may say) sworn brethren, that always jump together in a sinful society: her oath being taken (see the just judgment of God, she had not power to confess that truth which would have wrought her out of all suspicion, but utterly denying that which was so manifestly proved against her), the justices thought it requisite (till further proof could be had on this presumption) to bind her over to give answer at the next assizes.

When from assizes to assizes during the passage of four years she was compelled to appear, nothing being further found against her, but her own denial; whereupon the first demand, if she had made but this persuasion and satisfying answer, as Judge Daniel very worthily urged against her at the trial, that keeping an inn, she had many guests, and many children lay at her house, of which number (for aught she knew) that might be one, but who brought them, from whence they come, or whither they will, she is not bound to take notice of. This might have been some instance of her innocence, but so to deny a question, the truth of which was not of sufficiency to bear her, argues a suspicion and mistrust of herself, and proves her to be guilty.

But to the former matter, she having made her appearance at so many several assizes and sessions, and no instance against her but the former, it was thought at Lent Assizes last, she should have been dismissed the court: but in the meantime such is the just judgment of God, to the plague of murderers, and terror of them that delight in bad, the dumb shall speak ere they shall escape undiscovered.

For the dumb sister of this murdered child, for when she was in question, led (no question) four years up and down, from town to town, from country to country, by the hand of God was at Michaelmas last brought unto Hatfield, before whose coming thither, though Dell's wife was by the graver judgments held in some suspicion, yet was her honest carriage such to travelers and to all sorts of people she had to deal withall, that generally the whole country acquitted her, and held her of honest condition; for since the time of this murder it is credibly reported, that betwixt that and a hundred miles from thence, man's meat and horse meat[12] was not to be had so reasonable as then, nor to a traveler better usage.

Well the girl is come to Hatfield, and having been there two days straying from place to place, the third day she happened upon Dell's house, where, whether it were by especial note taken before, but rather truly to be judged by the divine instinct of heaven, to everyone that came by her, she would make such pitiful action, as would have pitied any reasonable creature to have beheld her, as tearing of her hair, pointing to her throat, stopping of her mouth, pointing to the woodstack, and in the motion hereof, shed tears as bitter as if her brother's former murder had been in present action.

This strangeness, noted through all the town, bred a wonder in the people, and the rather for that the girl by no means could be drawn from thence; at last the bailiff of Hatfield, taking advice with some of his brethren, consulted together how they might try whether the dumb did this as tending to the revelation of some concealed suit, or provoked thereunto by ignorance, and in searching many ways, at last it came in their minds, that their neighbor Dell's wife had of long been in question about a child, taken up in Bottomless Pond (some four years since) or thereabout, whereupon they agreed to question the girl upon what particulars they could best think upon to that purpose, and withall remembering that by command from the justices of the shire, they had reserved the murdered child's coat, and purposed to make trial, if her remembrance could take any knowledge of it, but first resolved to tempt her memory, by showing her divers others.

---

12. Horses' feed.

The girl brought into a parlor among them, they began first to ask her of her name, as is thy name Joan, Alice, Agnes, Frances, Bess, and ever as they spake her right name which was Elizabeth, she would laugh and rejoice, on the contrary, at the naming her wrong seem discontent.

They having thus a knowledge of her name, began to question her further, if she never had had a brother; when presently she (as she accustomed before) fell a weeping, making all the former signs in the former order; then they asked her what clothes he used to go in. She, to the best declaration she could, made signs thereof, whereupon they showed her many children's coats of several colors, and ever as she happened upon a green, that she would kiss, and cry, ever throwing all the rest from her, with so lovely and lively action, that they were confident the murdered boy was her brother. At last they brought to her the right coat, which after she had earnestly taken note of, the poor child grew to that vehement passion, as if in the sight thereof she had seen another brother murdered, when by no persuasion, offerings, gifts, nor no course that could be taken, to part from the coat, as if for the loss of a brother, she would keep it as a remembrance of him. All which signified to the justices and knights of the shire, the town had an especial charge to provide more carefully for her, and not to suffer her any longer to lie in the streets, and her brother's coat was given to her to wear out.

This wonder, the only table talk in the country, though often brought to the Widow Dell's ear, she made slight of it (persuading herself belike) that with her honest report and store of wealth, the child having not a tongue to utter anything in her reproof to wrest out of it, which (no question) she had done, notwithstanding all the arguments and instances against her. But for the wonderful works of God, an example able to make all people, that for desire of riches, honor, promotion, or what titles soever would be a murderer or consent thereunto, to loathe the thought thereof, even in the creation, and content themselves with their estate (how mean soever) rather than seek to rise by indirect means, knowing that a guilty conscience salamanderlike lives always in fire, that his days are dreadful, his nights terrible, that he that admits sin in himself, kills himself, that to unhonest pleasure is begot a companion repenting, and enrich himself with this saying, *"Somnia bonorum meliora quam malorum.*[13] And though I live poor, I live rich in this, that I am virtuous, I am not a Bondman to my thoughts, nor slave to my affections. *Nemo liber qui servit cupiditatibus."*[14]

This wench (as before is reported) being by the direction placed where she had relief, one day, some months before Christmas last, going to play with the goodwife's daughter where she sojourned in a park joining to Hatfield (commonly called the King's Park), as they were in sport together, a cock hard by them fell a crowing, when the other girl mocking the cock with these words, "Cocka doodle doo, Peggy hath lost her shoe," and called to her, "Bess, canst not thou do so?" When presently the girl in the like manner did so, which drawing the other child into amazement, she presently left her, and ran home crying out as she went, "The dumb girl Bess can speak, the dumb girl Bess can speak." The wonder caused all the town to gather in flocks, ran to meet her, but the bailiff and the constables (more discreet than the rest) kept the flurry from her. When she answered them to every question directly, and forthwith began in order to reveal the former murderers, as before is mentioned.

Speedy news was carried to all the chief men in the shire, who, driven into astonishment with the report, and the miraculous accident, that a child without a tongue should speak both discreetly and distinctly, to the revealing of so monstrous a murder, and by the crowing of a cock (that bird that put Peter in mind of his great sin in denying our Savior and his Master) was the herald to

13. "The dreams of good men are better than those of evil."
14. "No one is free who is a slave to greed."

proclaim to this child, when she should speak these things, that by her the wonderful works of God might be glorified, and the murders discovered.

But the lives of the king's subjects, and those which till then had been reputed honest, being now like to depend on her justification, the justices were very careful to sift her by several examinations, to see if they could find her alter or trip in any part of her former discourse, as Sir Ralph Conesbye, Sir Henry Butler, Master Auditor, and Master Auditor Curle, to the number of fourteen knights and grave gentlemen of note, justices of peace, took her several examinations, when in the general there could not be one found that differed in a syllable; nay though some of them threatened her with what vengeance God would stir up for her in hell, and plagues here upon earth, if she persisted to be a liar, and a murderer, both which would conclude in her (by the death of Dell's wife and her son) if she persevered in this testimony. Others in milder train dealt with her, as by fair persuasions, golden promises, that from the state of a beggar, where till then she had lived, she should now be exalted and maintained by them in the same degree as their own children, making them stand present objects to alter her, neither of which could make her distant in anything, but in brief satisfied them with this answer: "I must not lie; I have that within me bids me tell truth."

Notwithstanding this, one of Sir Henry Butler's men (to make a further trial of her constancy herein, watching her abroad in the same park where first her lost speech was revealed unto her) attired himself in a vizard[15] with horns and (as we commonly say) like a divell, and out of a thicket stepped before her, and threatened her, that in that place where she first spake, he would tear her in pieces for helping George Dell and his mother, when the girl (though in common it doth appear she should have been frightened from her constancy) only answered thus: "Good

---

15. Mask.

Gaffer Divell do not hurt me, I speak nothing but truth, and what
the thing within me instructeth me to speak." With the wonder
of this miracle (time passing away) people coming from all
places to be eye- and ear-witness thereof, the assizes were to be
held at Hartford, where (according as they were bound) George
Dell and his mother appeared, and being called to their trial (as
in form of law in such cases are provided) they pleaded not guilty.
When the girl (as boldly in accusing, as wonderful in speaking)
gave evidence against them, saying, that since God had lent her
a speech by miracle, she would with that inspired breath follow
the law of them, and have their bloods lawfully, who stole away
her brother. Dell's wife being yet asked by the judge whether
such lodged in her house or no, who yet continued her denial,
when the aforesaid Henry Whilpley, Nicholas Deacon, with
others, were ready to avow the being there besides many credible
persons of Hatfield, who in the life of her husband (being a
blind man, and living in great discontent together) hath often
heard him say: "Thou mayst rise a while, but a day will come
when thy villainies and murders will appear, when thy fall
shall be low enough." Upon this evidence (the jury going together) they were found guilty, and a verdict returned, whereupon the judge according to course proceeded in sentence against
them, where learnedly he instructed them, that since God had
revealed them murderers (as from the tongues of babes and
sucklings, that a child spake by miracle to her discovery, and
that accordingly they were cast by twelve credible men of their
own country), they would yet look into themselves, seeing how
near they were unto their graves, and make that more plain
which yet lay somewhat obscure, namely, who were partakers
with them in that bloody action. But nothing prevailing to
mollify their obdurate hearts, briefly thus they replied, "Since
the law hath cast us, we desire to die." Whereupon the second
of August being Saturday, having received their sentence, they

were conveyed to the gaol, where being permitted to be together as long as they had stay in this world, by a prisoner that lay over them, was heard this conference. "Mother," quoth George Dell, "the law hath cast me, and I am resolved for death. I pray for you (if you can) resolve the world, whether I am guilty or no." Who answered him, "Son, be contented, take thy death patiently, it is now too late, I have spoken what I will." The young son spending the time he had to live in prison in prayer and singing of psalms, that if the outward appearance may be a perfect witness in earnest repentance, till Monday the 4 of August, where being with his mother, by the jailor delivered to the sheriff, his mother having by suit obtained that she might see her son first suffer death, they were executed at the common place of execution, the young man (though the mother before this was beloved) the most lamented for.

The Crying Murther

"The Crying Murder" is a fascinating account of Elizabethan crime and punishment, rivaling in morbid interest the grisly Manson/Tate-Bianca murders of our time. A group of four—three men and a woman—were tried and executed for murdering, decapitating, disemboweling, and powdering a Mr. Trat, the curate at Old Cleeve, Somerset. Although the anonymous author of the pamphlet is certain that justice has been served in executing the four, the narrative raises some very interesting questions.

First of all, whose was the mangled body? Was it Trat, as the judges believed, or was it, as the defendants alleged, the body of a man whom Trat had murdered? Several people who had known Trat testified that they saw him after the murder; one of them even claimed that Trat had admitted stabbing a man and fleeing for his life. The author, and judges, believed that one of the murderers had dressed up as Trat, and had been able to fool Trat's old acquaintances into believing that they had seen the curate himself. This, needless to say, is questionable. Finally, there is the insistence of the defendants on their innocence. In a society in which virtually everyone believed that a repentant murderer would achieve salvation, but that one who remained obstinate in denying his sin would be damned, the fact that the defendants all denied the crime to the last casts some doubt on their guilt.

It was difficult to tell what happened at Old Cleeve in 1623; it is impossible to tell now. But it is interesting to speculate that a grave injustice may have been done. The defendants, however much they hated Trat, may have been innocent of his blood. And, it is possible that Trat did murder the traveler. Possibly he also pushed his wife from the cliff from which she allegedly fell. Then, with this double burden of guilt, he may have escaped, and under an assumed name emigrated to the wilds of New England, where he became a fire and brimstone preacher or a prosperous merchant, and the founder of a distinguished American family.

The crying Murther:

Contayning the cruell and most horrible Butcher of Mr. T R A T, Curate of olde *Cleaue* ; who was first murther as he trauailed vpon the high way , then was brought home to his hou and there was quartered and imboweld : his quarters and bowels being terwards perboyld and falted vp, in a most strange and fearefull manner. For this fact the Iudgement of my Lord chiefe Baron T A N F I E L D, young *Peter Smethwicke*, A drew Baker, Cyrill Austen, and *Alice Walker*, were executed this last Summer Assizes, the 24. of Iuly, at Stone Gallowes, neere Taunton in Summerset-shire.

AT LONDON:
Printed by *Edw: Allde* for *Nathaniell Butter.*
1 6 2 4.

Diverse foreign nations for those more open and known faults, which custom hath made remarkable amongst them, have by the note of your English censure suffered the common brand of infamy and reproach. Hence it is that most of our curious censurers, and some of them (not our least sinners) have taxed the French for lightness, the Dutch for drinking, the Danes for cruelty, the Italians for pride and covetousness, the Spaniards for delays and subtleties. But in vain do we lay these aspersions upon others, thereby to palliate our own disgrace, or seek to cover with these fig-leave garments our own deformity and nakedness. For many amongst us (as it is to be feared) are conscious of these, and of many other enormous sins besides, to let pass fearful atheisms, terrible blasphemies, tearing oaths, and unnatural lusts, which provoke the just vengeance and indignation of our Maker.

That lethargy of security doth so possess our spirits, that although we sleep with the serpent continually in our bosoms, yet we rest careless and secure of his dangerous temptations and designs. Covetousness is so hydropical[1] and longing amongst the purse-sick tympanists of this age, that like unto that idol of lust, the more they have, the more they still desire. And then what doth the generality of our nation do, who with such Catonian rigor do censure others?

> *Quaecunq, profunda*
> *Traxit avaritia, luxu peiore refundit.*

(What covetousness hath got, luxury doth spend in surfeit and excess.)

Our modern murders, which are their most raging where other sins are most reigning, seem equal, though not for the number, yet for the manner, unto these of the Mahometan

---

1. Dropsical.

assassins, men obliged thereto by their profession, or to the Italian banditos, people inured there by custom. The scarlet tincture and guiltiness whereof pollutes the earth, infects the air, and cries for vengeance at the gates of heaven, and the judgment seat of the Almighty. So that no more *Angli quasi Angeli*,[2] may these transgressors be called Angles or English, because we are like the Angels: but we may be called *Deires, quasi dei ira,* as being the anger of God, and the poured out lees of the cup of His indignation.

Amongst the list and number of which most horrid precedents, where of England like Libya, *Semper aliquid profert novi,* doth always produce new shapes and subjects, none have been more notoriously noted, and infamously famous, than those three assassinations committed with these few years in Summersetshire, on the north side of Quantock Hills: the first, of Thresher killed at St. Adries, by his own wife and her adulterous lover; the second, of Robert Seaman of Norton, butchered at Otterhampton by his brother-in-law Legge and his wife; and the last (which is the tragical subject of this present discourse) is the cruel and unheard of murder of Mr. Trat, curate of Old Cleeve in the said county, by young Peter Smithwicke's (as the law found it) accomplices and associates. For the better explanation whereof, we may methodically consider these five circumstances: first, the person murdered, and the persons murdering; secondly, the motives which did induce them to commit this murder; thirdly, the manner of committing and executing of it; fourthly, the means, and presumptive evidences, by which it was discovered; fifthly, the arraignment, judgment, and execution. Of all which considerations, several orders, according to that intelligence which I have received from credible persons, engaged in their trial.

---

2. The famous pun of Gregory the Great, who seeing fair-haired English captives in Rome, remarked that they were not Angles, but angels.

And first concerning the person murdered: he was a levite,[3] consecrated unto the Lord to do Him service in the tabernacle of his congregation; one that had many years since put on the breastplate of Urim and Thummim,[4] and girded himself with the linen ephod;[5] concerning which sort of people, the Lord doth give this injunction and charge by the pen of a ready writer, by the mouth of that kingly prophet David. "Touch not mine anointed, nor do my prophets any harm." Before he had taken this sacred order of priesthood upon him, he had spent some of his younger years in the University of Oxford, being a student of Magdalen College, where he proceeded Bachelor of Arts, with good approbation and allowance of his superiors: his moral conversation (both there and in the country) was honest and laudable; only some aspersions were laid upon him, by the known report of this malicious company, who first did seek to murder his good name, before they murdered and took away his life. From hence sprang this occasion: his wife (being a feeble, sickly, and weak woman) went to gather limpets (a kind of shellfish that sticks upon the rocks in that Sevearne or midland sea,[6] dividing England from Wales), and by an unfortunate chance fell from the precipice of the rocks into the water, and there upon the sudden perished, her husband being upon the strand also, but a good distance removed from her, as being employed in fishing at another place, so that he could not come to her succor in time.

Presently upon this accident, the poison of asps which was under his enemies lips broke forth into the running issue of a false report, and they noised it everywhere among the vulgar that Mr. Trat had killed his wife, and cast her over the rocks into

3. Deacon.
4. Mysterious sacred objects mentioned in Exodus (28:30) as being worn on the breastplate of the high priest.
5. Sleeveless priestly garment.
6. I.e., the estuary of the Severn River.

the sea. But this calumniation coming to the examination of the justices of that division, it was found to be counterfeit by the touchstone, and he was cleared without further trial, and his enemies departed with shame and rebuke. Another scandal which was laid upon him was this: he being by them invited unto supper, came according to appointment; where these plowers (according to the phrase of the Psalmist) plowed upon his back and made large furrows upon him, for one of the creatures, as it appeared afterward, took up the minister's gown and put it on; in which counterfeit habit (it being now dark night) he goes forth and meets with a country woman, unto whom he offers some violence and uncivil behavior. She guessing by the outside conjecture that it was Mr. Trat spreads this attempt abroad to his infamy and disgrace, which coming to his ears, he seeks to vindicate his reputation, and calls the actors of this plot into question, who were found to be guilty of the fact, and were punished by the censure and sentence of the court. Neither were his moral parts only commendable, but his ministerial also were unanswerable. For although he was none of the greatest clarks,[7] as they say, yet was he not a dumb pastor, but like a true Bonarges,[8] did thunder and cry out in his sermons against the vices of his parish: the freedom whereof, together with some particular applications unto young Smithwicke, was thought to be one of the chiefest causes which hastened this heinous and unheard of murder. And thus much for the quality of the person murdered.

The persons murdering who suffered for the fact, were four in number: young Peter Smithwicke, Andrew Baker, Ciril Austen, and Alice Walker, which persons although they were not blemished before the committing of this fact with the scandal of any notorious crimes, in the course of their former life and con-

---

7. Scholars.

8. Boanerges, surname given by Jesus to James and John; by extension, a loud and vociferous preacher.

versation, yet were they not free from the suspicion of some faults, whereof youth by nature, and age by custom is too guilty and capacious. But old Peter Smithwicke who is not yet come to his trial, but remains a prisoner in the gaol in Ilchester, was reputed by all men before the suspicion of this cruel assassination, so that if he should be guilty of this crime, as the most judicious judgments doubt,[9] although the vulgar people and his friends think the contrary, it may be said of him, which was said of another in the same kind, *cucullus non facit monachum,*[10] it is not the outside shew or shadow which makes the inward sanctimony and integrity. And thus much for the persons murdering. In the next place follows the consideration of those motives which did incite these men to imbrue their hands in the blood of the innocent, and these were supposed to be three in number: the first was Mr. Trat's liberty of speech in his usual and public rebuking of some of that society of some suspected passages of sin whereunto they were thought to be overweaningly addicted and accustomed. The next was the vindication of that reproach and infamy which they suffered by offering violence unto an honest woman in the counterfeit larva or image of Trat. But the last motive which was not the least, but the chiefest of all from whence this current of Meribah,[11] the first stream of this malice, did proceed was this: Mr. Brigandine of Quantock's Head in the said county of Somerset, being incumbent over the parsonage of Quantock's Head, and over the vicarage of Old Cleeve, where this innocent man now murdered was his curate for a good season, took a resolution to resign his incumbency of Old Cleeve unto his curate, who before had bought the patronage of it from him, upon conditions of a fitting value and consideration. With this young Smithwicke and his father were much distasted, as having held that vicarage of Cleeve, from

---

9. Fear.
10. "A cowl does not make a monk."
11. The place where Moses brought forth water from the rock.

Mr. Brigandine who married old Mr. Smithwicke's mother, at an undervalued rate and rent, by which means a good annual profit did accrue to his purse, of which revenue by this new contract he was like to be put off and defrauded as he gave out, for that he pretended a promise from his father-in-law Brigandine to the contrary, confirmed unto him many years since by the mediation of his mother. And his son Peter thought himself wronged in his case also, and that he was a fellow sufferer with his father in this calamity, because that Mr. Brigandine, his grandfather by marriage, had promised as he said, the perpetual donation and patronage of this living. Hence sprung the chiefest flame of that malice, which from the small sparks of mean or false suppositions caused such combustion in the household of Mr. Smithwicke to the utter ruin of their credits, estates, and lines, and to the final peril of their souls, they dying to the world's esteem obstinate and unrepenting sinners, without acknowledging their guiltiness in the fact whereof they were so plainly guilty by the conjecture of all outward proofs and circumstances. But from hence let us descend unto the manner of it, which was most tragical, horrid, and inhumane, wanting an imitable precedent and example, even amongst the very pagans and infidels. So that

> *Quis talia fando*
> *Mirmidonum Dolopumve, aut duri miles Vlissis*
> *Temperet a lachrimis?*[12]

What heart can be so inhumanely inhumane and obdurately hardened which would not sigh at the very repetition of it, and yearn at the remembrance of this cruel and scarlet-colored assassination? For these bloodsuckers having murdered this harmless levite Mr. Trat, upon the Wednesday next after Mid-

---

12. "Who in telling such things, either Myrmidon or Dolopian, even the stern Ulysses, would not be moved to tears" (*Aeneid*, Book 2).

summer Day[13] in the year of our Lord God 1623, journeying from his own house to his mother's whither he went to furnish his necessities with some money, they brought him back the next night thus murdered as he was with two mortal wounds in the breast unto his own dwelling house again, where he lived solitary and alone. There these butchers, with their hands already smoking in his blood, did cut up his carcass, unbowel and quarter it; then did they burn his head and privy members, parboil his flesh and salt it up, that so the sudden stink and putrefaction being hindered, the murderers might the longer be free from discourse. Master Trat having now been missed fortnight and a day, and there being a great stench smelt from his house by the neighborhood, which now began to be noisome notwithstanding the drying force and operation of the salt, by the direction and advice of the next officers, they broke up the doors, and gained their passage in: where having made a diligent search and inquiry they find his foresaid body, all saving the head and members, disposed in this manner and form following. His arms, legs, thighs, and bowels were powdered up into two earthen steens or pots in a lower room of the house, close adjoining unto the wall, the bulk of his carcass was placed in a vat or tub, covered over with a cloth in a chamber overhead, all which members thus dissevered were so artificially jointed, laid, and handled, that if these devils had been butchers they could not have done it more orderly and cunningly. Besides this, near unto this spectacle there was an old green suit found belonging as it is likely unto one of the actors of this murder which afterwards was carried about to the next market town and cried publicly, but as yet it could never find out an owner or a master.

This murder being evident in the fact and heinousness thereof, though doubtful in the person, because his head and members could not be found, they presently give notice unto Mr. Thomas

13. June 24.

Windham of St. Decumans, unto Master Cuffe of Creech, justices of peace in the said country, who with Mr. John Westcombe of Haulgh, coroner for the king, came upon their first summons, and taking view of this strange and amazing object, they were much perplexed, and troubled in their minds, not knowing what to think at first, in a matter so strange and unheard of for the example. Yet collecting their spirits from doubtfulness and confusion, unto that course which the necessity of the cause did impose upon them, they proceeded from thence unto examination of some of the neighbors in that parish, the intelligence of whose report might give their eyes some informing light in the mystery of this business. Those examinates make it known unto them that in all likelihood it was Mr. Trat their old curate that was murdered, there being one of his fingers known by a secret mark unto them, and besides, there was a known quarrel between Mr. Smithwicke's company and him, in respect of the causes before premised, which gave some cause of suspicion unto them, and that Alice Walker besides, servant unto old Mr. Smithwicke, had before told some of these informers, that if the parson did not come home the sooner, his powdered beef would stink before his coming. These presumptions drew her first of all unto question and examination before the justices, who were very sincere and careful in the finding out of this murderous and butcherly plot. She being taxed, stood upon the denial, but there being great presumptions of her guiltiness, she was committed unto prison. Old Mr. Smithwicke upon this, seeing his servant imprisoned, his son suspected, and himself something blemished, protested openly concerning their innocence, and his adversary's malice, offered large bail for his maid, sent (as he noised it amongst the vulgar) for his absent and innocent son to London, and rode in a progress of inquest after[14] Trat, whom he thought to be the murderer of this un-

---

14. Conducts a search for.

known person, and not the person that was murdered by him or any of his company. To make this good, upon that day when Trat was thus massacred, there was one that in his habit and cloak usurped his name, and came to John Ford's house of Taunton the bowyer,[15] a man who had seen Trat, but did scarce know him, or now remember him, and told him that he was M. Trat, the curate of Old Cleeve, and passed under that name there. The like he did at Ilminster, and at Parson Sacheverel's, a minister, beneficed near Blanford in Dorsetshire, who had been formerly and familiarly acquainted with Trat in Oxford, though now by means of their long absence, this counterfeit did presume that he had forgotten him, and for his consideration, was confident, that being habituated thus like Trat, and countenanced alike besides, he might therefore with more facility impose upon the credulous ignorance of Sacheverel.

To further this project, which might free Smithwicke and his household from all suspicion, and lay the guilt of the murder upon the murdered, this imposter, calling at his pretended friend's house in the dusk of the evening, told him, that he was his old friend Trat, which now after many years was come to see him. The other being deceived with the night, his boldness and habit, believed his words, and desired him to alight, but he refuseth it, alleging that he could not do it with a personal safety. "And for the reason?" said the other. "Because," quoth the counterfeit, "I have stabbed a man in my house where I live, of whose life I am doubtful; and that upon this occasion coming from Dunster, a small market town in the northeast part of Summersetshire, I met with one, newly as he told me, came out of Ireland, who begging something of me, I gave him two pence, lodged him in my own house, gave him his supper and his breakfast in the morning, but crossing himself superstitiously, as I thought, with the sign of the cross before his morning's meal, I

15. I.e., John Ford, the bowyer (man who makes bows), of Taunton.

taxed him for it: who seeking to maintain his cause by argument, we fell from words to blows, and in the combat, I doubt[16]
that with a stab of my knife, I have killed him, and so being
engaged in this danger, I can stay no longer with you, but must
fly." Sacheverel wished him to retire himself home again since
he was not certain or well assured of this stranger's death, and
that by chirurgery[17] and speedy means of relief, the wounded
person might again recover his former health and vigor. Old
Smithwicke being thought to be conscious of all these counterfeit false designs, as diverse men now think and suspect, he
pursued the inquest of this false Trat, enquires for him at Ford's
the bowyer's his first place of arrival: who told Master Smithwicke, that such a man was there, but departed then to Ilminster
as he thought, because he inquired the way thither of him. The
other follows him by his track unto the town of Ilminster, and
from thence unto Sacheverel's house in Dorsetshire, there inquiring for him of the parson; he was told by him that Mr. Trat
was there, but would not alight nor stay with him any time, because he had stabbed a man in his own house (as he said) of
whose safety he was very doubtful, and suspicious.

The persons accused, being armed with these glozes[18] and
pretenses, fair seeming to the eyes of rash speculation and beholding, condemn Mr. Windham and Mr. Cuffe of injustice,
protested of their wrongs before Mr. Sims and Mr. Brureton,
two other justices of that county, and desired them in the king's
behalf to take the examination of old Ford and others of his
household concerning Mr. Trat, whether he were there upon
such a day or no in his house with him, how long he stayed, and
whether as he thought from thence he departed. And they required and requested them besides to use their best means and
authority unto the justices of peace in Dorsetshire, that Mr.

16. Fear.
17. Surgery.
18. Tricks.

Sacheverel might be examined upon the same interrogatories also. But all these fair pretenses proved at the trial but clouds of cunning and mists of knavery for Ford, his man, and Sacheverel being pressed unto it, first by the justices, and after by my Lord Tanfield, Lord Chief Baron of the Exchequer, would not take their oaths, nor at last give assurance by their words that this person was that Trat indeed, although they confessed themselves in respect of the forged premises very doubtful of it at first. These passages made pregnantly against those persons, who have suffered for the murder, and give great presumptions against old Smithwicke, whose trial is deferred till the next assize of that county.

Those other proofs which gave most evidence against them may be reduced unto two kinds, unto general ones, which did concern them all, in general, or particular ones, which did concern every one of them severally by himself. The proofs general against them were these: first of all, the personal counterfeiting of Mr. Trat; 2. The reins of Trat's bridle, known by his brother and found at Smithwicke's house all bloody, his horse upon which he rode forth, being never heard of till this day; 3. The finding of diverse pieces of the skull and neckbone, with some teeth on Smithwicke's hearth, answerable unto those which were found in Trat's own house. It being thought by the judge and jurors that his head was first burned at Smithwicke's and after that the bones and teeth were carried unto Trat's, all saving those fragments which God would have for the further manifestation of the truth, concealed in the foresaid hearth, until they were found out by the industrious care and search of Mr. Cuffe and Mr. Windham. The proofs particular were different against diverse of them. Young Peter Smithwicke had often threatened to cut him to pieces, to kill him, and to show him such a trick as was never heard of in Summersetshire; and besides riding to London a little before the fact, for he was not present at it except it were by suggestion. He wisheth a friend of his with whom he encountered withal to take notice that he was in London upon such a day, upon which the murder was afterward known to be committed. Those against Alice Walker, being a maidservant unto Smithwicke, were these: she threatened him and gave it out that if the priest had come to the last Dunster Fair, he should have been cut as small as herbs to the pot by her countryman the Welshman.

Again, after the murder was committed, but not detected, she gave it out, that if he did not come home the sooner, his powdered beef would stink, as after that his powdered flesh did indeed very shortly. But this horrible assassination being detected, and she not suspected, she came out of the guilty burthen of her own conscience unto one of her neighbors, and taxed her for accusing of her, concerning Mr. Trat's death, who protested unto her that, which she afterward made good unto the justices, that she never spake it in her lifetime, nor at that present so much as thought it.

The presumptions against Andrew Baker were these: his usual conversation and familiarity at Smithwicke's house, his voluntary throwing down of a pot of stinking blood, supposed to be Trat's, which was hidden behind rue and other strong-smelling herbs at Mr. Smithwicke's, which pot he was commanded to take out very carefully, by the justices then present, and last of all, his usual crying and calling out in his sleep, "Let us fly, Mr. Peter; let us away or else we shall be all undone and hanged."

That which made against Ciril Austin was this: after this murder was committed, he comes to Woolavington, a parish twelve miles distant from Old Cleeve, and gets entertainment as a day laborer, amongst the neighborhood. Being there at work, amongst other of his fellows, there was one brought word of this most cruel butchery from Bridgewater, but reported withal that the manner of it was not yet well and fully known: "What," says Austin, "I can tell you it was thus and thus," and relates all the particulars of it, for who could relate it better, than he that did commit it? Besides he had about him a bloody napkin, which being without question imbrued in the blood of the innocent, he plucks this gored as it was out of his pocket, to wipe his face withal.

There being a maid present, demands of him, why he did not wash his handkerchief, and by what means it became so bloody. He makes her no direct answer; but presently tears it in two pieces, and buries them with trampling in the dirt.

Upon this Austin grows suspicious amongst the neighborhood, and flies withal upon the jealousy of their suspicion, and his own guiltiness, which they apprehending, inform Master Cuffe of Creech, of all these passages who hunts after him with the hue and cry, but could not apprehend him, but though he ran like Cain from the presence of man, yet mark how the finger of God doth fasten on him; for flying into Wilshire, he come unto one Master Long's a justice of peace in that country, and begs some relief at the door of a young gentlewoman, born near unto him, and that had heard of this Austin's attainture,[19] which he did under the name of Ciril Austin. She informs Mr. Long of it, he stays this suspected person and draws him into examination concerning the murder committed at Cleeve and those passages delivered at Woolavington by him, of which Mr. Long had heard at large by others. Austin stands upon the denial, and Mr. Long commits him upon this to the gaol, where he aggravates the suspicion by another circumstance; for being visited by some acquaintance in prison, he tells them upon an occasion of paying for the reckoning, that he wanted no monies, and if he did, others there were that should smoke for it: which words were thought to be meant of young Smithwicke consider-

19. Implication in the crime.

ing the reasons before premised. And thus much be spoken of those presumptive evidences which in general or particular did make against these men.

In the last place follows their arraignment, indictment, and execution, for the clearer expression whereof, you must conceive thus much: that this murder being committed in the year of our Lord God 1623, the morrow after Midsummer Day, my Lord Chief Baron Tanfield deferred the trial of it until these last summer assizes 1624. But then the truth by time growing more perspicuous, for *Veritas Temporis Filia,*[20] and young Peter Smithwicke by the working power of God's providence being come in, and Ciril Austin being apprehended in Wilshire, to satisfy the longing expectation of all men, whose eyes were fastened upon the issue of this matter, he proceeds unto the trial in a direct and most judicious manner: for having perused their several examinations, to avoid all partiality which consanguinity or acquaintance might impose, his lordship alters the whole body of the Grand Jury, which were for the most part of the western parts of Summersetshire, and therefore in likelihood of most known acquaintance unto Master Smithwicke who sometimes had been a Grand Jury man himself. Then after weightiness of the cause proposed, and charge given with great sufficiency and integrity, the Grand Jury was dismissed and commanded to their charge, who after a tedious balancing of the evidence, and a mature pondering of those proofs which were alleged in the bill of indictment, find young Peter Smithwicke, Andrew Baker, Ciril Austin, and Alice Walker guilty of Mr. Trat's murder, but find an *ignoramus*[21] of old Mr. Smithwicke's bill, who was recommitted unto the gaol of Ilchester, to the intent that time might produce stronger proofs against him, which I could wish with diverse other men, might fail in his behalf. The Petty Jury[22]

---

20. "Truth is the daughter of time."
21. Legal Latin: "we take no notice of it."
22. A jury that tries the final issue of fact in civil or criminal proceedings.

concurs with them in verdict, and there were found guilty of this horrible and heinous assassination young Peter Smithwicke, Andrew Baker, Ciril Austin, and Alice Walker. Upon this my Lord Chief Baron proceeds to their judgment, and passing the sentence of death upon them, he gives them godly admonitions to confess the murder, plain enough by the proofs and evidence, and by this means to give God and the world public satisfaction. But they standing stiff upon the negative, and their own pretended innocency, they are sent back from the court, unto the ward again, where they were visited by Dr. Goodwin, Dr. Slaier, Mr. Morley, Mr. Vaughn, and other worthy ministers, who with all zeal did exhort them to clear their consciences, and confess their faults with true repentance. But all these wholesome admonitions, proved but seed sown in stony ground, for it took no root nor impression in them; only Alice Walker told Mr. Morley, who required her to confess the truth, and demanded of her whether or no they had obliged themselves by oath or vow unto the contrary; she, I say, then tells him that he in that spake somewhat to the purpose, and desires a farther conference with him in the morning. He charitably comes unto her, and pressing her upon her former words, desires this Alice in the bowels of our Savior to confess her fault, notwithstanding any wicked vow or protestation made by her, or her accomplices, for such vows were not to be observed, but only good ones and such as were made unto the Lord, but the evil spirit working strongly with her made her insensible of these good and godly motions; and she returns *ut canis ad vomitum,* like a dog unto the ancient vomit of her stubbornness and denial. On Friday being the twenty-fifth day of July, they were conveyed from the town of Taunton unto Sloan Gallows about eleven of the clock in the forenoon where notwithstanding all the persuasions used by some of the aforesaid divines, they suffered by the hand of justice, died obstinate and unrepenting sinners. The causes wherefore they would not confess were thought to be these: first, the obligation of their vow; 2. the conceived fear of a more terrible punishment; 3. the hope of impunity or a reprieval at the last, since as they thought the proofs were not sufficient against them. Concerning this event men's conjectures were diverse: for those who were allied unto them, either in consanguinity or acquaintance, were of partial judgment in their behalfs, and thought them innocent; because they protested their innocency at their deaths, others whose judgments were more sincere, and curious considering those pregnant proofs which made against them, thought them justly punished by the censure and judgment of the court. The golden use which we may gather from this black and bloody precedent is this: that we should not give the reins unto anger for fear it gives the reins and law to us; and though wrongs either true or supposed may give provocation, yet we should consider withal that *Plus nocitura est ira quam iniuria,* that anger may hurt us more than the injury, drawing us many times (except we prevent it with wisdom and discretion) from wrath to malice, from malice to revenge, from revenge to murder. And therefore I will conclude this sad discourse with the poet's wholesome saying: *Ira furor brevis est: animum rege; qui nisi paret, imperat; hunc frenis, hunc tu compesce catena.*[23]

---

23. "Anger is a brief madness: rule your spirit, which unless it obeys you, commands you; check it with curbs, with chains" (Horace, Epistles I, 2, 62–63).

The Murder of
Page of Plymouth

The account of the murder of Page of Plymouth is a natural for Elizabethan tragedy: a woman, forcibly married to a man she does not love, plots with her lover to kill her husband. The murder was a grisly one; after strangling Page with his own kerchief, the murderers broke his neck against the bedstead. They then stuck him in bed and smoothed the bedclothes to look as if he had died quietly in his sleep. Marks of violence on the corpse gave the murderers away, and they were tried and executed.

This pamphlet seems pretty certainly to have been a major source of Thomas Dekker and Ben Jonson's tragedy, *Page of Plymouth,* performed by the Admiral's Men in 1599. The play, unfortunately now lost, was what scholars today generally refer to as a *murder play*—a tragedy based on a recent crime involving common people. The anonymously written *Arden of Feversham* (1591) is the best-known play of this sort. Thomas Yarrington's *Two Lamentable Tragedies* (1594) and the anonymous *A Warning for Fair Women* (1599) are other examples.

THE MURDER OF PAGE OF PLYMOUTH*

Of Master Page of Plymouth, murthered by the consent of his own wife, with the strange discovery of sundry other murthers.

* From "Sundry Strange and Inhumane Murders, Lately Committed." See frontispiece for title page.

Wherein is described the odiousness of murther, with the vengeance which God inflicteth on murtherers.

In the town of Testock, ten miles or thereabouts from Plymouth, there dwelled one M.[1] Glanfeeld, a man of as good wealth and account as any occupier[2] in that country. This M. Glanfeeld favored a young man named George Strangewidge, who was of such great credit with him that he turned over all his wares, shop, and dealings into his hands, and took so good liking of him being a proper young man that it was supposed he should have had his daughter in marriage, and the rather for that he had learned the full perfection and knowledge of his trade in London, in the service of a worshipful citizen called M. Powell in Bredstreet, and grew so painful and seemed so good a husband as the said M. Glanfeeld's daughter did wholly resolve that the said Strangwidge should be her husband and no other. Whereto in troth her parents never did condescend. But Satan, who is the author of evil, crept so far into the dealings of these persons that he procured the parents of mislike of Strangwidge and to persuade the daughter to refrain his company, showing her that they had found out a more meeter match for her, and motioned unto her that it was their pleasures she should marry one M. Page of Plymouth, who was a widower, and one of the chiefest inhabitants of that town, and by reason that the said M. Glanfeeld did mean to abide at Plymouth, he thought it a more sufficient match to marry her in Plymouth, where she might be hard by him, than to marry her to Strangwidge who dwelt far from him. In the end such was the success that although she had settled her affection altogether upon Strangwidge, yet through the persuasion of her friends[3] though sore against her will, she was married to M. Page of Plymouth, notwithstanding that she had protested never to love that man

---

1. *M.* is the abbreviation for *Master,* the Renaissance equivalent of *Mister.*
2. Dealer or merchant.
3. In this context, *friends* means close relatives.

with her heart, nor never to remove her affection settled upon said Strangwidge, which she performed as the sequel maketh manifest: for this Mistress Page had access to Strangwidge and he to her at his coming to Plymouth, whereby the Devil so wrought in the hearts of them both, that they practiced day and night how to bring her husband to his end. And thereupon the said Mistress Page as appeareth since by her own confession, did within the space of one year and less, attempt sundry times to poison her husband, for it was not full a year, but that she had procured him to be murthered, as you shall hear immedi- ately.

But God who preserveth many persons from such perils and dangers, defended still the said M. Page from the secret snares and practices of present death, which his wife had laid for him, yet not without great hurt unto his body, for still the poison wanted force to kill him, so wonderfully did God work for him, yet was he compelled to vomit blood and much corruption, which doubtless in the end would have killed him, and that shortly. But to prosecute and that with great speed to perform this wicked and inhuman act, the said Mistress Page and Strang- widge omitted no opportunity. They wanted no means nor friends to perform it for their money, whereof they had good store, and more than they knew how to employ, except it had been to better uses. For she on the one side practiced with one of her servants named Robert Priddis, whom as she thought nothing would more sooner make him pretend[4] the murdering of his master than silver and gold, wherewith she so corrupted him, with promise of sevenscore pounds more, that he solemnly undertook and vowed to perform the task to her contentment.

On the other side Strangwidge hired one Tom Stone to be an actor in this tragical action, and promised him a great sum of money for performing the same, who by a solemn vow had

---

4. Intend, plan.

granted the effecting thereof, though to the hazard of his own life.

These two instruments wickedly prepared themselves to effect this desperate and villainous deed upon the eleventh of February, being Wednesday, on which night following the act was committed, but it is to be remembered that this Mistress Page lay not then with her husband, by reason of the untimely birth of a child whereof she was newly delivered, the same being dead born, upon which cause, she then kept her chamber, having before sworn that she would never bear child of his getting that should prosper, which argued a most ungodly mind in the woman, for in that fact she had been the death of two of her own children.

About ten of the clock at night M. Page, being in his bed slumbering, could not happen upon a sound sleep, and lying musing to himself, Tom Stone came softly and knocked at the door, whereupon Priddis, his companion, did let him in, who was made privy to this deed, and by reason that Mistress Page gave the straight charge to dispatch it that night whatsoever came of it, they drew toward the bed, intending immediately to go about it, M. Page being not asleep as is aforesaid, asked who came in, whereat Priddis leapt upon his master being in his bed, who roused himself and got out upon his feet, and had been hard enough for his man, but that Stone flew upon him being naked, and suddenly tripped him, so that he fell to the ground, whereupon both of them fell upon him, and took the kercher from his head, and knitting the same about his neck, they immediately stifled him. And as it appeareth even in the anguish of death, the said M. Page greatly labored to pull the kercher from about his neck, by reason of the marks and scratches which he had made with his nails upon his throat, but there he could not prevail, for they would not let slip their hold until he was full dead. This done, they laid him overthwart the bed, and against the bedside broke his neck, and when they saw he was surely dead, they stretched him and laid him in his bed again, spreading the clothes in ordinary sort, as though no such act had been attempted, but that he had died on God's hand.

Whereupon Priddis immediately went to Mistress Page's chamber and told her that all was dispatched. And about one hour after he came again to his Mistress' chamber door and called aloud, "Mistress," quoth he, "let somebody look into my master's chamber, me thinks I hear him groan." With that she called her maid, who was not privy to anything, and had her light a candle, whereupon she slipped on her petticoat and went thither likewise, sending her maid first into the chamber, where she herself stood at the door, as one whose conscience would not permit her to come and behold the detestable deed she had procured.

The maid simply felt on her master's face, and found him cold and stiff and so told her mistress, whereat she had the maid to warm a cloth and wrap it about his feet, which she did, and when she felt his legs, they were as cold as clay, whereat she cried out, saying her master was dead.

Whereupon her mistress got her to bed, and caused her man Priddis to call her father, M. Glanfeeld, then dwelling at Plymouth, and sent for one of her husband's sisters likewise, willing her to make haste if ever she would see her brother alive, for he was taken with the disease called the *pull* as they term it in that country. These persons being sent for, they came immediately, whereat Mistress Page arose and in counterfeit manner sounded,[5] whereby there was no suspicion a long time concerning any murder performed upon him, until Mistress Harris his sister spied blood about his bosom, which he had with his nails procured by scratching for the kercher when it was about his throat. Then they moved his head, and found his neck broken,

---

5. Swooned.

and on both his knees the skin was beaten off, by striving with them to save his life.

Mistress Harris, hereupon perceiving how he was made away, went to the mayor and the worshipful of the town, desiring them of justice, and entreated them to come and behold this lamentable spectacle, which they immediately performed, and by searching him, found that he was murdered the same night.

Upon this the mayor committed Priddis to prison, who being examined, did impeach Tom Stone, shewing that he was a chief actor in the same. This Thomas Stone was married upon the next day after the murther was committed and being in the midst of his jollity, suddenly he was attacked and committed to prison, to bear his fellow company.

Thus did the Lord unfold this wretched deed, whereby immediately the said Mistress Page was attached upon the murther and examined before Sir Francis Drake, Knight, with the mayor and other magistrates of Plymouth, who denied not the same, but said she had rather die with Strangwidge than to live with Page.

At the same time also the said George Strangwidge was newly come to Plymouth, being very heavy and doubtful, by reason he had given consent to the said murder, who being then in company with some of London, was apprehended and called before the justices for the same, whereupon at his coming before them, he confessed the truth of all and offered to prove that he had written a letter to Plymouth before his coming thither, that at any hand they should not perform the act. Nevertheless M. Page was murdered before the coming of this letter, and therefore he was sent to prison with the rest unto Exeter and at the assizes holden this last Lent, the said George Strangwidge, Mistress Page, Priddis, and Tom Stone, were condemned and adjudged to die for the said fact, and were all executed accordingly upon Saturday being the twentieth day of February last, 1591.

Other Strange Things Seen at That Time

Upon the same night and three nights after, there was seen an ugly thing formed like a bear, whose eyes were as it had been fire, bearing about him a linen cloth representing the instrument wherewith the said M. Page was murdered.

Also in Plymouth the same week in the presence of sundry honest persons, was visibly seen a raven, which did alight upon the head of a ship's mast, sunk at the end of the town. This raven standing upon the top of the mainmast, did with her talents[6] pluck up certain rope yarns that hung down from the head of the mast, and fastened them about her neck and often turned them about her neck with all her force, which done, she plunged herself right down, clapping her wings close to her body, and never left until she had hanged herself.

Now the ship was all this while aground, lying with her stern to the shore, and suddenly the said ship turned herself round and brought her stem where erst her stern did lie, all which are strange, yet is the same so true, as it cannot be disproved, being justified by those that saw the same.

The Lord bless us, and give all other grace to be warned by these examples and inhuman actions before recited: that we may avoid the danger of shedding of innocent blood, and fear the judgment of God which continually followeth willful murderers. Eternal God preserve this little island, bless the Queen's Majesty, and her honorable council, turn thy wrath always from us, O Lord, and pour down thy blessings upon her Highness, that she our Moses, may long live to hold up the Tables of the Law in her gracious hands, and that we may seek continually to please her in such due sort as she may have no just cause to throw them down, which God grant for his mercy sake. Amen.

---

6. Talons.

Murder upon Murder

"Murder upon Murder," like most ballads about contemporary crimes, is printed in two parts, each on a separate broadside. Both parts are illustrated with crude, lurid woodcuts depicting scenes from the murderers' careers.

Ballads were written in verse, and set to music. It may seem odd to a modern reader that these early analogues to our news stories were done that way, but it is not surprising when one recalls that the first literature of most cultures is poetry, not prose, and that it is generally chanted or sung. The reason is probably mnemonic. Before printing and widespread literacy, literature was oral, and rhythm, rhyme, and tune are great aids to memory. Accordingly, it is understandable that the ballad was initially the chief medium for describing important events in England. By the 1580s, as printing entered its second century and literacy had greatly increased, the prose pamphlet, with its ability to treat subjects at greater length and in more detail, replaced the ballad as the chief news medium.

The meter and stanzaic pattern of the ballad vary in accordance with the tune to which it is set. The tune used here, "Bragandary," was a popular one, and a number of other ballads of murders were set to it.

MURDER UPON MURDER

Murder upon murder, committed by Thomas Sherwood, alias, Country Tom, and Elizabeth Evans, alias, Canbery Bess, the first upon M. Loe; the second of M. George Holt of Windsor, whom inhumanely they killed near Islington on the twenty-

second day of January, 1635; the last upon M. Thomas Claxton
of London, mercilessly they murdered upon the second day of
April last past, near unto Lamb's Conduit on the backside of
Holborn, with many other robberies and mischiefs by them
committed from time to time since midsummer last past, now
revealed and confessed by them, and now according to judgment
he is hanged near to Lamb's Conduit this fourteenth of April,
1635. To the terror of all such offenders. To the tune of "Bragandary Downe," etcetera.

List Christians all unto my song,
'Twill move your hearts to pity,
What bloody murders have been done,
Of late about the city:
We daily see the blood of Cain,
Amongst us ever will remain.
O murder, lust and murder,
Is the foul sink of sin.

There scarce a month within the year,
No murders vile are done,
The son, the father murdereth,
The father kills the son,
Twixt man and man there's much debate,
Which in the end brings mortal hate,
O murder, lust and murder,
Is the foul sink of sin.

The mother loseth her own life,
Because she her child doth kill,
And some men in their drunkenness,
Their dear friends blood doth spill,
And many more, through greedy gain,

Murder upon Murder,

Committed by *Thomas Sherwood*, alias, *Countrey Tom*: and *Elizabeth Evans*, alias, *Canbrye Besse*: The first upon M. *Loe*, The 2. of M. *George Holt* of *Windzor*, whom inhumanely they kild neare *Islington* on the 22.day of January 1635. The last upon M. *Thomas Claxton* of *London*, whom mercilefly they murdered upon the fecond day of Aprill laft paft, neare unto Lambs Conduit on the back-fide of Holborne, with many other robberies and mifchiefes by them committed from time to time since Midfomer iaft paft, now revealed and confeft by them, and now according to Judgement he is hangd neare to Lambs Conduit, this 14 of Aprill, 1635.to the terror of all fuch offenders.

To the tune of Bragandary downe, &c.

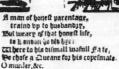
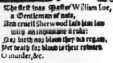

All Chriſtians all vnto my ſong,
will moue your hearts to pitty,
that blody murthers haue bene done,
here about the City:
betly ſee the bꝛood of Cain,
ſhall be euer will remaine.
murder, luſt and murder,
the foule ſinke of ſin.

It's ſcarce a moneth within the yeare,
if murthers vile are done,
When the father murthereth,
a father kills the ſon,
twixt man and man there's ſuch debate,
which in the end bꝛings mortall hate.
murder, &c.

The mother loſeth her owne life,
caule ſhe her child doth kill,
ſome men in their dꝛunkenneſſe,
their deare friends blood doth ſpill,
ſonny moꝛe,thꝛough greedy gaine,
bꝛother hath the bꝛother ſlaine.
murder, &c.

The ſtoꝛy now in hand,
truth I will declare,
God ſeanch mind vnto himſelfe,
that then beware,
both Sherwood truely ſayde,
to murder bent his mind.
&c. &c.

A man of honeſt parentage,
traind vp to husbandry,
But weary of that honeſt life,
to London go old hie:
There to his diſmall woefull Fate,
he choſe a Queane foꝛ his copeſmate.
O murder, &c.

One Canbery Beſſe in Turnball-ſtreet,
on him did caſt an eye,
And pꝛayd him to giue her ſome dꝛinke,
as he was paſſing by:
So the two ſoone be gan conſent,
And foꝛ the ſame now repent.
O murder, &c.

Foꝛ by alluring temptings bates,
the ſotten ſo his minde,
That vnto any villany,
fierce Sherwood was incline,
His coyne all ſpent he muſt haue moꝛe,
Foꝛ to content his filthy (whoꝛe)
O murder, &c.

Such miſchiefe then by them it was done
in and about the City,
But ſtill they ſcape vnpuniſhed,
(not knowne) moꝛe was the pitti,
To deatly ſinnes they then did fall,
not onely robbe but murder all.
O murder, luſt and murder,
is the reall deuil let in.

The firſt was Maſter William Loe,
a Gentleman of note,
And cruell Sherwood laid him low
with an inqueant a robe:
foꝛ birth noꝛ bloud they did regard,
yet death foꝛ blood is their reward.
O murder, &c.

One Maſter Holt of Winſor towne,
a Neiowich fates be,
Walking abꝛoad to take the ayre,
fell next their butchery,
foꝛ Sherwood with a fatall blow,
This yeoman kill'd, his queane and ſe,
O murder, &c.

His cloak, hat, ruffe from him they do
reform great alſo,
One were about his cloathes to ſtripe,
his ſhirt, ſhoes, hoſe throwe,
But being feard, away they got,
he hath content this villany.
O murder, &c.

I vile loſe life they ſtill run on,
regarding no fleare or,
their hearts ſtill bent to crueltry,
not minding to ſalvati..
they cannot be ſatiſ..fi'd the two
that begg..
O murder, &c.

The second part   To the same tune.

For being flusht with humane bloud,
they thirsted still for more,
The more from God O man thou runst
the greater is thy score:
Like rauening wolues they pry & watch,
How they the innocent may catch.
O murder, lust and murder,
is the foule sinke of sin.

The last that fell into their hands,
was Master Claxton he,
A Gentleman of good descent,
and well belou'd truely,
Who walkt warm'd by breake of day,
In holborne fields they did him slay.
O murder, &c.

A scarlet coate from him they tooke,
new sut from top to toe,
His bootes, hat, shirt they tooke from him
much money else also,
And left him in the fields so wide
So fled away and not discride.
O murder, &c.

But marke the goodnesse of the Lord,
on the succeeding day,
That Sherwood with his trull did think
beyond sea take their way,
In Dounditch were together tane,
Selling the coat in the same lane.
O murder, &c.

With the new sut vpon his back,
and all things else beside,
The queane the hat of Master Holt,
which they had murdered,

A W

So vnto Newgate were they sent,
Confest all this, and doe repent.
O murder, &c.

Wishing all men when as they walke
to haue a speciall care,
And not to go vnarm'd, or late,
but sway'd by truncheon ware,
Had they done so Sherwood both say,
He had not ventred them to slay.
O murder, &c.

Within three quarters of a yeare,
these murders they haue done,
And maim'd and spoiled many a one,
by their confession:
Such deadly blowes he did them giue,
T'was strange that after they should liue
O murder, &c.

For these bad facts he now doth dye,
iust iudgement for his murder,
All such ill liuers grant they may,
no worse nor better spead,
So shall England from crying straine,
Be euer freed, God mercy winne.
For murder lust and murder,
is the foule sinke of sinne.

FINIS.

Printed at London for T. Langley,
and are to be sold by Thomas Lambert
in Smithfield, neere to the Hospitall
gate.

The brother hath the brother slain.
O murder, lust and murder,
Is the foul sink of sin.

Of the story now at hand,
The truth I will declare,
How God leaves man unto himself,
Of Satan then beware,
Thus doth Sherwood truly find,
He unto murder bent his mind.
O murder, lust and murder,
Is the foul sink of sin.

A man of honest parentage,
Trained up to husbandry,[1]
But weary of that honest life,
To London he did hie:
Where to his dismal woeful fate,
He chose a quean[2] for his copesmate.[3]
O murder, lust and murder,
Is the foul sink of sin.

One Canbery Bess in Turnbull Street,
On him did cast an eye,
And prayed him to give her some drink
As he was passing by;
O so too soon he gave consent,
And for the same doth now repent.
O murder, lust and murder,
Is the foul sink of sin.

---

1. Farming.
2. Whore.
3. Colleague.

For by alluring tempting baits,
She sotted so his mind,
That unto any villainy
This Sherwood was inclined,
His coin all spent he must have more,
For to content his filthy whore.
O murder, lust and murder,
Is the foul sink of sin.

Much mischief then by them was done,
In and about the city,
But still they escape unpunished
(Not known) more was the pity,
To deadly sins they then did fall,
Not only rob but murder all.
O murder, lust and murder,
Is the foul sink of sin.

The first was M.[4] William Loe,
A gentleman of note,
And cruel Sherwood laid him low
With an inhuman stroke:
Nor birth nor blood they did regard,
Yet death for blood is their reward.
O murder, lust and murder,
Is the foul sink of sin.

One M. Holt of Windsor Town,
A Norwich factor[5] he,
Walking abroad to take the air,
Felt next their butchery,

---

4. Master.
5. Merchant who buys for others for a commission.

For Sherwood with a fatal blow,
This goodman killed, this quean willed.
O murder, lust and murder,
Is the foul sink of sin.

His cloak, hat, ruff, from him they took,
Eleven groats also,
And were about his clothes to strip,
His shirt, shoes, hose thereto,
But being scared, away they hie,
He has confessed this villainy.
O murder, lust and murder,
Is the foul sink of sin.

A vile loose life they will run on,
Regarding not their end,
Their hearts still bent to cruelty,
Not minding to amend:
They cannot see Satan the Devil,
That drags them into all this evil.
O murder, lust and murder,
Is the foul sink of sin.

The second part, to the same tune:

For being flushed with human blood,
They thirsteth still for more,
The more from God and man
Thou runst the greater is thy score:
Like ravening wolves they pry and watch,
How they the innocent may catch.
O murder, lust and murder,
Is the foul sink of sin.

The last that fell into their hands
Was M. Claxton he,
A gentleman of good descent
And well beloved truly,
Who walked unarmed by break of day,
In Holborn fields they did him slay.
O murder, lust and murder,
Is the foul sink of sin.

A scarlet coat from him they took,
New suit from top to toe,
His boots, hat, shirt they took from him,
Much money eke[6] also,
And left him in the fields so wide
And fled away and not descried.
O murder, lust and murder,
Is the foul sink of sin.

But mark the goodness of the Lord,
On the succeeding day,
That Sherwood with his trull did think
Beyond sea take their way,
In Houndsditch were together tane,[7]
Selling the coat in the same lane.
O murder, lust and murder,
Is the foul sink of sin.

With a new suit upon his back,
And all things else beside,
The quean the hat of M. Holt,
Which they had murdered,
So unto Newgate were they sent,

6. In addition.
7. Taken, captured.

Confessed all this, and do repent.
O murder, lust and murder,
Is the foul sink of sin.

Wishing all men when as they walk
To have a special care,
And not to go unarmed, or late,
But sword or truncheon wear.
Had they done so, Sherwood doth say,
He had not ventured them to slay.
O murder, lust and murder,
Is the foul sink of sin.

Within three quarters of a year
These murders they have done,
And maimed and spoiled many a one,
By their confession:
Such deadly blows he did them give,
It was strange that after they should live.
O murder, lust and murder,
Is the foul sink of sin.

For these bad facts he now doth die,
Just judgment for his meed.
All such ill-livers grant they may,
No worse nor better speed,
So shall England from crying sin,
Be ever freed, God's mercy win.
O murder, lust and murder,
Is the foul sink of sin.

Finis

Printed at London for T. Langley, and are to be sold by
Thomas Lambert in Smithfield, near to the Hospital gate.

Witchcraft

If the ideas of our Shakespeare students about the Weird Sisters in *Macbeth* are at all typical, there seems to be a widespread belief in America that witches are imaginary creatures something on the order of trolls or elves—that is, they do not exist, nor have they ever existed. On the contrary, however, witches did, and indeed still do, exist. A witch is, simply, a man or woman who worships the Devil. Devil worship was *the* defining factor in traditional medieval and Renaissance definitions of witchcraft, and if we can trust the public prints,[1] this is still the case in Southern California, where the black arts flourish today.

Here, for example, are some typical Renaissance descriptions of witches. William Perkins wrote in 1608: "A witch is a magician, who either by open or secret league, wittingly and willingly, consenteth to use the aide and assistance of the Devil, in the working of wonders." Perkins emphasizes that the second part of the description is the part "wherein standeth the very thing, that maketh a witch to be a witch: The yielding of consent (to the Devil) upon convenant."[2] James Mason, writing in 1612, describes witches as: "liege people which have given as it were their names unto him [the Devil] to serve him."[3] And in "A Confirmation and Discovery of Witchcraft" (1648), John Stearne calls witchcraft the most atrocious of crimes because witches "renounce God and Christ, and give themselves by a covenant to the Devil."

Confessions and contemporary accounts give overwhelming evidence that people did worship the Devil in Renaissance England. In short, as far as the Renaissance is concerned, there can be no question of "believing" in witches. For an Elizabethan, not believing in witches would

---

1. See, e.g., the series of articles in *Esquire*, March 1970, pp. 99–122.
2. "A Discourse of the Damned Art of Witchcraft," 1608, p. 3.
3. "Anatomy of Sorcery," 1612, p. 6.

have been like not believing in Puritans—he might not approve of them, but he would not deny their existence. Whether Elizabethans treated witches humanely or cruelly is, of course, another question.

The practice of witchcraft is a venerable one. Margaret Murray traces witchcraft back to the ancient cult of the Horned God, which has its roots in beliefs of the Paleolithic period.[4] George L. Kittredge asserts, "There is scarcely a single item of malefic witchcraft in Elizabethan annals that cannot be matched in the beliefs of the ancient Assyrians."[5] But whatever the ultimate origin, it is clear that witchcraft as practiced in Renaissance England was not a sophisticated cult with a distinct set of theological doctrines and practices; it was simply a grim parody of Christianity. Witches, like Christians, believed in God, the Devil, angels, demons, prayers, and rituals: they took whatever the Christians held to be good as evil, and whatever Christians abhorred as their good. Christians prayed to God; witches prayed to the Devil. Christians abhorred sin (or believed they should, at any rate); witches reveled in it. Their attitude toward the Christian world was that of the Weird Sisters: "Fair is foul and foul is fair."

What made Renaissance witches nay-sayers? Some educated witches may have had a Faustian fascination with evil, but among the lower classes, which produced most of the witches, the main factor was the frustration of the powerless. This probably also explains why so many witches were women—in Renaissance England there was no more powerless creature than a poor, old woman.

Renaissance accounts of witches reveal a recurrent pattern. A downtrodden and despised woman is mistreated by a more fortunate and powerful neighbor, and strikes back the only way she can—by cursing her tormentor and making some vague threat. A short time later some misfortune befalls the neighbor, and the woman is haled into court as a witch. The accused often believes herself guilty, and confesses. She tells how she stuck pins in a wax doll, for instance, or chanted evil incantations. The whole proceedings may seem ridiculous to us, but in a day when medicine was primitive, and superstition prevalent, it is easy to see how the sudden death of a child or a pig could be attributed to witchcraft.

Here are a few of many accounts of this sort of situation. Mother

4. *The God of the Witches* (Essex, 1962).
5. *Witchcraft in Old and New England* (New York, 1929), p. 27.

Sutton, an aged hogherd of Milton, fell out with a farmer named Enger. She swore revenge on Enger, and allegedly cast spells on his livestock and servants. Enger's seven-year-old boy threw stones at her and called her a witch. Mother Sutton was furious at the child. When shortly afterward the boy sickened and died of a mysterious illness, Mother Sutton was apprehended, convicted, and executed.[6]

Joan Vaughan, a Northhampton lass of low birth, bandied insults one day with a gentlewoman named Belcher. Mrs. Belcher slapped her. Joan muttered threats, and several days later Mrs. Belcher was "suddenly taken with . . . a griping, and gnawing in her body." She blamed Joan, continually crying out, "Here comes Joan Vaughan; away with Joan Vaughan."[7]

Elizabeth Fraunces was convicted of fatally bewitching Andrew Byles for refusing to marry her.[8] Joan Peterson allegedly afflicted Christopher Wilson so that he raved and fell into fits because he refused to pay her for tending him during an illness.[9] Joan Cunny, a widow of eighty, confessed making a boy lame for stealing a load of wood.[10] And, so it went.

Witches often testified that the Devil offered his services at their hour of need. The Devil seldom appeared himself; he usually sent a spirit. These spirits might take human form: Joan Wallis of Keyston confessed seeing a man in black, called, appropriately enough, Blackeman. He frightened her because he had "ugly feet," and because he would "sometimes seem to be tall, and sometimes less, and suddenly vanished away."[11] More commonly the spirits were animals—dogs, cats, pigs, toads, or strange hybrids. The spirit that appeared to John Winnick was "black and shaggy, having paws like a bear, but in bulk not fully so big as a coney [rabbit]."[12]

If the person approached became a witch, the spirits remained as attendants or *familiars*. The witch allowed them to suckle extra teats that appeared on her body. These familiars generally had colorful names like Grizzel, Greedigut, Trillibub, Beelezebub, and Vinegar Tom.

---

6. "Witches Apprehended, Examined and Executed," 1613.
7. "The Witches of Northamptonshire," 1612.
8. "A Detection of Damnable Drifts," 1579.
9. "The Witch of Wapping," 1652.
10. "The Apprehension and Confession of Three Notorious Witches at Chelmsford," 1589.
11. "The Witches of Huntingdon," 1646, p. 12.
12. Ibid., p. 3.

Official concern with witchcraft goes back in England at least as far as the eighth century. In 747 the Council of Clevesho directed bishops to warn their parishioners that God's law forbids "soothsayers, auguries, auspices, amulets, spells, and all the filth of impious errors of the heathen."[13] The oldest secular law against witchcraft, that of King Alfred (849–99), is also based on God's law: "These women who are wont to receive enchanters and magicians and wizards or witches—thou shall not suffer them to live." This is an obvious echo of Exodus 22:18: "Thou shalt not suffer a witch to live." The tenth-century law of Edward and Guthrum and the eleventh century law of Aethelred forbade witchcraft on pain of death or banishment.[14]

One death penalty for witchcraft was recorded in the tenth century: a woman was drowned in London for driving nails into an image of her husband.[15] But capital punishment for witchcraft was rare in the Middle Ages, although the death penalty was common for a variety of offenses that we would consider petty—shoplifting, for instance. The more usual punishment for witchcraft was prison or the pillory. For instance, in 1406 Henry IV wrote to the Bishop of Lincoln complaining of the wizards and sorcerers in the diocese, and ordered him to round them up and imprison them until they "abandoned their arts."[16]

However, when Elizabeth took the throne in 1558, the situation changed radically. Parliament drew up a bill, finally passed in 1563, decreeing the death penalty for all who "use, practice or exercise invocations or conjurations of evil and wicked spirits to or for any intent or purpose."[17] This was vigorously enforced. In 1566 Agnes Waterhouse was convicted of witchcraft, and put to death. Although records are incomplete, evidence indicates that during the remainder of Elizabeth's reign (until 1603), approximately fifty others were executed.[18]

James I, Elizabeth's unpopular successor, has gone down in history as a monster who murdered hundreds, or even thousands, of innocent old women.[19] The evidence, incomplete as it is, indicates that he was no worse than Elizabeth—that is, about forty witches were executed during

13. Kittredge, *Witchcraft*, p. 27.
14. Ibid.
15. Ibid., p. 29.
16. Ibid., p. 59.
17. Ibid., p. 282.
18. Wallace Notestein, *A History of Witchcraft in England 1558–1718* (New York, 1911), p. 56.
19. Kittredge, *Witchcraft*, pp. 276–77.

his reign.[20] This is bad enough, of course; it may be argued that one execution is too many. But in a time when even the best of monarchs put people to death for the flimsiest of reasons—petty theft, political opposition, hair-splitting heresy—it seems unfair to single out James for special opprobrium. Furthermore—and this is not intended as exculpation, either—it should be noted that the evidence also indicates that James was thoroughly in line with the wishes of his subjects in the matter of these executions. Like the bulk of his subjects, James believed that witches committed murder by diabolic magic, and he favored prosecuting them like any other murderers.

Trials and executions continued throughout the Parliamentary period and the Restoration. The last execution for witchcraft in England probably took place at Exeter in 1682.[21] Although the common people hated witches as much as ever, judges were no longer inclined to give credence to their accusations. The publication in 1718 of Francis Hutchinson's skeptical *Historical Essay on Witchcraft* ended forever the persecution of witches in England.

The pamphlet "The Apprehension and Confession of Three Notorious Witches" contains the confessions of three witches executed at Chelmsford, Essex, in 1589: Joan Cunny, Joan Prentiss, and Joan Upney. Despite our modern skepticism about witches and witchhunts, it seems likely that the confessions are genuine. That is not to say that the events described actually happened, but that the ladies in question testified voluntarily that they did. Of course, it is possible that someone connected with the court made up the confessions, and the women simply signed them. However, everything we know about the period leads us to believe that the judges conducting the trials were men of integrity. They were badly misguided on the question of how much harm a witch could do, but that does not mean that they would allow the fabrication of evidence in order to get a conviction.

In short, it seems likely that Mother Cunny and the others did attempt to inflict injury by using powers they believed the Devil had lent them, and that they confessed in order to escape cruel punishment in the next world at the cost of encountering it in this.

---

20. Ibid., pp. 228, 328.
21. Notestein, *Witchcraft in England,* p. 313.

¶ The Apprehension and confession

of three notorious Witches.

Arreigned and by Iustice condemned and

executed at *Chelmes-forde*, in the Countye of
Essex, *the 5. day of Iulye, last past.*

1 5 8 9.

¶ With the manner of their diuelish practices and keeping of their
spirits, whose fourmes are heerein truelye
proportioned.

IOAN PRENTIS
& hir Bid

IACKE

GILL

Imprinted at London for Edward Allde. 1589.

One of the most interesting parts of the pamphlet is the description
of the witches' imps: Mother Cunny's black frogs, Jack and Jill; Joan
Prentiss's ferret, Bidd; and Mother Upney's mole and toad. These imps

would seem to be the product of the power of suggestion on a diseased imagination. Imps traditionally appeared to witches; these witches would have expected them. The casual sighting of a rat or toad could easily be exaggerated into an elaborate tale of an imp.

THE APPREHENSION AND CONFESSION OF THREE NOTORIOUS WITCHES

To the reader:

If we would call to remembrance the manifold mercies and innumerable benefits which the Almighty hath and daily bestoweth upon us, in consideration thereof, we are bound to withdraw our filthy affections and naughty dispositions, from the use of such detestable dealings, as both are detested of God, whose almighty commandments forbideth them, and unto man, whose laws are constituted to punish them as odious before the sight of God, whereon our earthly laws groundeth and consisteth and therefore used to punish or cut off such lewd or filthy offenders as by breaking the divine decrees of the Almighty, by the laws of man deserves to be condemned. But such is the blindness of our estate, the naughtiness of our affections, and the desire of our devilish appetites, that neither the commandments of God, the laws of our realm, the love of our neighbors, our own welfare, or the fall of others can or may move us to consider how profitable it were for us to examine our lives, and to blemish such vices in us as both the laws of God and man forbiddeth: For what can be more odious or abominable unto God than the deprivation of his divine power, by yielding ourselves serviles unto Satan for a little worldly wealth, or hatred we have to our neighbors, where we might rest the servants, nay the sons of Almighty God, who sent His only Son to redeem us from the servitude of bondage, and to bring us unto His bliss and eternal felicity, which shall evermore remain perfect, which if we would consider, what Christian is so blinded with ignorance or overcome with illusions of Satan, but he would tremble to think upon the judgments of the Almighty pronounced against such offenders of the laws of the realm, which by justice deceiveth them from their devilish practices and abominations? The glory whereof, although it be secretly concealed and used, yet cannot long continue, because the Almighty will be no partaker of any such dealings, nor the heart of any faithful Christian conceal the secrets thereof: which for example I have here published unto you the discourse of such devilish practices as have been used by notorious witches, whose names and actions I have severally touched in the treatise following: with the manner of their accusations, taken and approved before both honorable and worshipful Her Majesty's justices, at the last assizes holden at Chelmsford in the county of Essex, according to the copies both of the offenders' confession by examination and their accusations registered.

THE ARRAIGNMENT AND EXECUTION OF JOAN CUNNY OF STISTED IN THE COUNTY OF ESSEX, WIDOW, OF THE AGE OF FOURSCORE YEARS, OR THEREABOUTS, WHO WAS BROUGHT BEFORE ANTHONY MILDEMAY, ESQUIRE, THE LAST DAY OF MARCH, 1589.

In primis,[1] this examinant saith and confesseth that she hath knowledge and can do the most detestable art of witchcraft, and that she learned this her knowledge in the same, of one Mother Humphrey of Maplested, who told her that she must kneel down upon her knees, and make a circle on the ground, and pray unto Satan the chief of the devils, the form of which prayer that she then taught her, this examinant hath now forgotten, and that then the spirits would come unto her, the which she put in practice about twenty years since, in the field of John

---

1. First of all.

Wiseman, of Stisted, Gentlemen, called Cowfen Field, and there making a circle as she was taught, and kneeling on her knees, said the prayer now forgotten, and invocating upon Satan: two spirits did appear unto her within the said circle, in the similitude and likeness of two black frogs, and there demanded of her what she would have, being ready to do for her what she would desire, so that she would promise to give them her soul for their travail, for otherwise they would do nothing for her. Whereupon she did promise them her soul, and then they concluded with her to do for her what she would require, and gave themselves several names, that is to say the one Jack, the other Jill, by the which names she did always after call them. And then taking them up, she carried them home in her lap and put them in a box and gave them white bread and milk.

And within one month after she sent them to milk Durrell's beasts, which they did, and they would bring milk for their own eating and not for her.

And further, she saith that her spirits never changed their colors since they first came unto her, and that they would familiarly talk with her, when she had anything to say or do with them, in her own language.

And likewise she confesseth that she sent her said spirits to hurt the wife of John Sparrow the Elder, of Stisted, which they did, and also that where Master John Glasscock of Stisted, aforesaid, had a great stack of logs in his yard, she by her said spirits did overthrow them.

And further, saith that she hath hurt divers persons within this sixteen or twenty years, but how many she now knoweth not.

Furthermore, she confesseth that she send her spirits in to William Unglee of Stisted, miller, and because they could not hurt him, she sent them to hurt one Barnaby Griffin, his man, which they did. Likewise she confesseth, that she sent her said spirits to hurt Master Kitchen, minister of the said town, and also unto one George Coe of the said town, shoemaker, to hurt him likewise: but they could not, and the cause why they could not, as the said spirits told her, was because they had at their coming a strong faith in God, and had invocated and called upon Him, that they could do them no harm.

And further she saith, that Margaret Cunny, her daughter, did fall out with Father[2] Nurrel, and gave him cursed speeches, and thereupon, she thinketh she sent her spirits to her. Also she doth utterly deny that she sent her said spirits to Finch's wife, Devenish's wife, and Reynold Ferror or any of them to hurt them.

And being further examined, she confesseth that although her said spirits at some time can have no power to hurt men, yet they may have power to hurt their cattle.

This Joan Cunny, living very lewdly, having two lewd daughters, no better than naughtypacks,[3] had two bastard children. being both boys; these two children were chief witnesses, and gave in great evidence against their grandam and mothers, the eldest being about ten or twelve years of age.

Against this Mother Cunny the elder boy gave in this evidence which she herself after confessed, that the going to Braintye Market, came to one Harry Finch's house, to demand some drink, his wife being busy and abrewing, told her she had no leisure to give her any. Then Joan Cunny went away discontented: and at night Finch's wife was grievously taken in her head, and the next day in her side, and so continued in most horrible pain for the space of a week, and then died.

Mother Cunny confessed that she sent her spirit Jill to torment her.

The same boy confessed that he was commanded by his

---

2. Respectful title given to an old and venerable man—no religious significance here.
3. Women of bad character.

grandmother to fetch a burden of wood, which he gathered, but another boy stole it from him, and he came home without: and told his grandam: and she commanded her spirits to prick the same boy in the foot, which was done, and the same boy came to the bar lame and gave evidence against her.

Again the same boy confessed that his grandam, when he had lost his wood, said she would have wood enough: and bade him go unto Sir Edward Huddleston's ground, being high sheriff of the shire, and to take with him Jack the spirit, and so he did, who went unseen to anybody but the boy, and when they came to a mighty oak tree, the spirit went about it, and presently the tree flew up by the roots: and no wind at all stirring at this time: which Master High Sheriff acknowledged to be blown down in a great calm.

THE CONFESSION OF JOAN UPNEY OF DAGENHAM, IN THE COUNTY OF ESSEX, WHO WAS BROUGHT BEFORE SIR HENRY GREY, KNIGHT, THE THIRD OF MAY, 1589.

This examinant saith, that one Justian Kirtle, otherwise called "White-cote," a witch of Barking, came to her house about seven or eight years ago, and gave her a thing like a mole, and told her that if she ought anybody ill will, if she bid it, it would go clap them.

She saith that mole tarried not above a year with her, but it consumed away, and then she gave her another mole and a toad, which she kept a great while, and was never without some toads since till her last going away from her house, when she confesseth she ran away, because she heard John Herald and Richard Foster say she was a witch and such other words.

She saith that one day she left a toad under the groundsill[4] at Herald's house, and it pinched his wife and sucked her till she died, but it never came to her the said Joan Upney again.

---

4. Threshold.

She saith that one day another toad went over her threshold as Richard Foster's wife was coming that way, and it pinched her, and never returned again.

Other two toads she left at home, when she ran away, but they consumed away. She saith that her eldest daughter would never abide to meddle with her toads, but her youngest daughter would handle them, and use them as well as herself.

THE EXAMINATION OF JOAN PRENTISS, ONE OF THE WOMEN OF THE ALMSHOUSE[5] OF HINNINGHAM SIBBLE, WITHIN THE SAID COUNTY: BEING TAKEN THE TWENTY-NINTH OF MARCH, IN THE THIRTY-FIRST YEAR OF THE REIGN OF OUR SOVEREIGN LADY ELIZABETH.

In primis, the said examinant saith and confesseth that about six years last past, between the feast of all saints, and the birth of our Lord God, the Devil appeared unto her in the almshouse aforesaid, about ten of the clock in the nighttime, being in the shape and proportion of a dunnish-colored ferret, having fiery eyes, and the said examinant being alone in her chamber, and sitting upon a low stool, preparing herself to bedward: the ferret standing with his hinder legs upon the ground, and his forelegs settled upon her lap, and setting his fiery eyes upon her eyes, spake and pronounced unto her these words following, namely: "Joan Prentiss give me thy soul," to whom this examinant, being greatly amazed, answered and said: "In the name of God, what art thou?" The ferret answered, "I am Satan, fear me not, my coming unto thee is to do thee no hurt but to obtain thy soul, which I must and will have before I depart from thee." To whom the said examinant answered and said, that he demanded that of her which is none of hers to give, saying: that her soul appertained only unto Jesus Christ, by whose precious blood shedding, it was bought and purchased. To whom the said

---

5. House for the aged poor founded by a private charity.

ferret replied and said, "I must then have some of thy blood," which she willingly granting, offered him the forefinger of her left hand, the which the ferret took into his mouth, and sitting his former feet upon that hand, sucked blood thereout, and so much that her finger did smart exceedingly: and the said examinant demanding again of the ferret what his name was: it answered, "Bidd," and then presently the said ferret vanished out of her sight suddenly.

Item, the said examinant saith further, that about one month after, the said ferrett came unto her in the nighttime as she was sitting upon a little stool, preparing herself to bedward, as is above said: "Joan wilt thou go to bed," to whom she answered, "Yea that I will by God's grace," then presently the ferret leapt up upon her lap, and from thence up to her bosom, and laying his former feet upon her left shoulder, sucked blood out of her left cheek, and then he said unto her, "Joan if thou will have me do anything for thee, I am and will be always ready at thy commandment," and thereupon she being a little before fallen out with William Adams his wife[6] of Hinningham Sibble aforesaid, willed the ferret to spoil her drink which was then in brewing, which he did accordingly.

Item, the said examinant furthermore saith and confesseth, that the said ferret diverse times after appeared unto her always at the time when she was going to bed, and the last time he appeared unto her was about seven weeks last past, at which time she going to bed, the ferret leapt upon her left shoulder, and sucked blood out of her left cheek, and that done: he demanded of her what she had for him to do? To whom she answered, "Go unto Master Glasscock's house, and nip one of his children a little, named Sara, but hurt it not," and the next night he resorted unto her again, and told her that he had done as she willed him: namely, that he had nipped Sara Glasscock, and

6. I.e., William Adam's wife.

that she would die thereof, to whom she answered and said, "Thou villain, what hast thou done? I bid thee to nip it but a little and not to hurt it, and hast thou killed the child?" Which speech being uttered, the ferret vanished away suddenly, and never came to her sithence.[7]

Item, she affirmeth, that the occasion why she did will her ferret to nip the child, was for that she being the day before at the house of the said Master Glasscock, to beg his alms, answer was made to her by one of his maidservants, that both her master and mistress were from home, and therefore desired her to be contented for that time, and thereupon the examinant departed greatly discontented, and that night sent her ferret to nip the child as is abovesaid.

Item, she saith and affirmeth, that at what time soever she would have her ferret do anything for her, she used these words, "Bidd, Bidd, Bidd, come Bidd, come Bidd, come Bidd, come suck, come suck, come suck," and that presently he would appear as is aforesaid: and suck blood out of her left cheek, and then performed any mischief she willed or wished him to do for her unto or against any of her neighbors.

Lastly, the said examinant saith and confesseth, that one Elizabeth Whale, the wife of Michael Whale of Hinningham Sibble aforesaid, laborer, and Elizabeth Mott, the wife of John Mott of the said town, cobbler, are as well acquainted with her Bidd as herself is, but knoweth not what hurt they or any of them have done to any of their neighbors.

When their indictments were read, and their examinations also, they stood upon their terms, to prolong life: yet to make the matters more apparent, sundry witnesses were produced to give evidence against them, and first the judge of the circuit very wisely with a great foresight called in the two bastard chil-

---

7. Since.

dren before mentioned, and commended them greatly for telling the truth of that which he should ask them, concerning their grandam and their mothers, which they did, and having said what they could, together with the depositions of sundry other witnesses, they having confessed sufficient matter to prove the indictment. The jury found these bad women guilty in that they had slain men, women, and children, and committed very wicked and horrible actions, diverse and sundry times, and thereupon, the judge proceeded, and pronounced the sentence of death against them, as worthily they had deserved.

After they had received their judgments, they were conveyed from the bar back again to prison, where they had not stayed above two hours, but the officers prepared themselves to conduct them to the place of execution: to which place they led them, and being come thither, one Master Ward, a learned divine, being desired by the justices, did exort these wicked women to repentance, and persuaded them that they would show unto the people the truth of their wickedness, and to call upon God for mercy with penitent hearts. And to ask pardon at his hands to the same: some few prayers they said after the preacher, but little else: more than this, that they had deserved to die, in committing those wicked sins: and so took their deaths patiently.

Note, that Mother Upney being inwardly pricked and having some inward feeling and conscience cried out saying: that she had grievously sinned, that the Devil had deceived her, and that she had twice given her soul to the Devil, yet by the means of God's spirit working in her, and the pains which Master Ward took with her, she seemed very sorry for the same, and died very penitent, asking God and the world for forgiveness even to the last gasp, for her wicked and detestable life.

Finis.

THE
Discovery of Witches:

IN
Answer to severall QUERIES,

LATELY

Delivered to the Judges of Assize for the
County of NORFOLK.

And now published

By MATTHEVV HOPKINS, Witch-finder.

FOR
The Benefit of the whole KINGDOME.

EXOD. 22. 18.
Thou shalt not suffer a witch to live.

LONDON,
Printed for R. Royston, at the Angell in Ivie Lane.
M. DC. XLVII.

THE DISCOVERY OF WITCHES

Matthew Hopkins (d. 1647), a lawyer at Ipswich and Manningtree, was a zealot who acted as a "witch-finder" from 1644–47—that is, he traveled from town to town examining local suspects to determine whether or not they were witches. As a result of his labors, sixty women were hanged in Essex, forty at Bury, and others at Norwich and in Huntingdonshire.

In 1646 John Gaule, vicar of Great Staughton, published a pamphlet, "Select Cases of Conscience Touching Witches and Witchcraft," exposing Hopkins as a charlatan.

Hopkins wrote a threatening letter to Gaule, and published this pamphlet to answer the questions Gaule had raised with his procedures. The defense was unsuccessful; Hopkins was tried, convicted, and hanged in 1647.

Zealots like Hopkins appear with depressing regularity in the course of history, but it must be remembered that they often reflect the wishes of the people. Whatever malevolence he possessed, Hopkins would have been powerless without the collaboration of the people of the towns he visited. What he said of himself was undoubtedly true: "He never went to any town or place, but they rode, writ, or sent for him. . . . "

When a people became uneasy and suspicious, superhunters arise to lead the persecution. Hopkins was a Renaissance forebear of men like Lavrenti Beria, whose secret police purged Russia of millions of imaginary enemies, and Joseph McCarthy, who fortunately was unable to have anyone killed, but who nonetheless ruined scores of lives in America's twentieth-century witch-hunts.

CERTAIN QUERIES ANSWERED, WHICH HAVE BEEN AND ARE LIKELY TO BE OBJECTED AGAINST MATTHEW HOPKINS, IN HIS WAY OF FINDING OUT WITCHES.

Query one. That he must needs be the greatest witch, sorcerer, and wizard himself, else he could not do it.

Answer. If Satan's kingdom be divided against itself, how shall it stand?

Query two. If he never went so far as is before mentioned, yet for certain he met with the Devil, and cheated him of his book, wherein were written all the witches' names in England, and if he looks on any witch, he can tell by her countenance what she is, so by this, his help is from the Devil.

Answer. If he had been too hard for the Devil and got his book, it had been to his great commendation, and no disgrace at all: and for judgment in physiognomy, he hath no more than any man else whatsoever.

Query three. From whence then proceeded this his skill? Was it from his profound learning, or from much reading of learned authors concerning that subject?

Answer. From neither of both, but from experience, which though it be meanly esteemed of, yet the surest and safest way to judge by.

Query four. I pray where was this experience gained? And why gained by him and not by others?

Answer. The Discoverer never traveled far for it, but in March, 1644, he had some seven or eight of that horrible sect of witches living in the town where he lived, a town in Essex called Maningtree, with diverse other adjacent witches of other towns, who every six weeks in the night (being always on the Friday night) had their meeting close by his house, and had their several solemn sacrifices there offered to the Devil, one of which this Discoverer heard speaking to her imps one night, and bid them go to another witch, who was thereupon apprehended, and searched by women who had for many years known the Devil's marks, and found to have three teats about her, which honest women have not: so upon command from the justice, they were to keep her from sleep two or three nights, expecting in that time to see her familiars, which the fourth night she called in by their several names and told them what shapes, a quarter of an hour before they came in, there being ten of us in the room, the first she called was

1. Holt, who came in like a white kitling.

2. Jarmara, who came in like a fat spaniel without any legs at all; she said she kept him fat, for she clapped her hand on her belly, and said he sucked good blood from her body.

3. Vinegar Tom, who was like a long-legged greyhound, with a head like an ox, with a long tail and broad eyes, who when this Discoverer spoke to, and bade him go to the place provided for him and his angels, immediately transformed himself into the shape of a child of four years old without a head, and gave half a dozen turns about the house, and vanished at the door.

4. Sack and Sugar, like a black rabbit.

5. Newes, like a polecat.

All these vanished away in a little time. Immediately after this witch confessed several other witches, from whom she had her imps, and named to divers women where their marks were, the number of their marks, and imps, and imps' names, as Elemanzer, Pyewacket, Peckin the Crown, Grizzel Greedigut, etc., which no mortal could invent; and upon their searches the same marks were found, the same number, and the same place, and the like confessions from them of the same imps (though they knew not that we were told before), and so peached[1] one another thereabouts that joined together in the like damnable practice, that in our hundred[2] in Essex, twenty-nine were condemned at once, four brought twenty-five miles to be hanged, where this Discoverer lives, for sending the Devil like a bear to kill him in his garden, so by seeing diverse of the men's paps, and trying ways with hundreds of them, he gained this experience, and for aught he knows any man else may find them as well as he and his company, if they had the same skill and experience.

Query five. Many poor people are condemned for having a pap, or teat about them, whereas many people (especially ancient people) are and have been a long time troubled with natural warts on several parts of their bodies, and other natural excrescences, as hemorrhoids, piles, [caused by] childbearing, etc., and these shall be judged only by one man alone, and a woman, and so accused or acquitted.

Answer. The parties so judging can justify their skills to any, and show good reasons why such marks are not merely natural, neither that they can happen by any such natural cause as is before expressed, and for further answer for their private judgments alone, it is most false and untrue, for never was any man

---

1. Accused.
2. Subdivision of a county, having its own court.

tried by search of his body, but commonly a dozen of the ablest men in the parish or elsewhere, were present, and most commonly as many ancient skillful matrons and midwives present when the women are tried, which marks not only he and his company attest to be very suspicious, but all beholders, the skilfullest of them, do not approve of them, but likewise assent that such tokens cannot in their judgments proceed from any of the above mentioned causes.

Query six. It is a thing impossible for any man or woman to judge rightly on such marks; they are so near to natural excrescences, and they that find them durst not presently give oath they were drawn by evil spirits, till they have used unlawful courses of torture to make them say anything for ease and quiet, as who would not do? But I would know the reasons he speaks of; how, and whereby to discover the one from the other, and so be satisfied in that.

Answer. The reasons in brief are three, which for the present he judges to differ from natural marks; which are:

1. He judges by the unusualness of the place where he finds the teats in or on their bodies, being far distant from any usual place, from whence such natural marks proceed, as if a witch plead the marks found are hemorrhoids, if I find them on the bottom of the backbone, shall I assent with him, knowing they are not near that vein, and so others by childbearing, when it may be they are in the contrary part?

2. They are most commonly insensible, and feel neither pin, needle, awl, etc. thrust through them.

3. The often[3] variations and mutations of these marks into several forms confirms the matter; as if a witch-finder (as they call him) is coming, they will, and have put out their imps to others to suckle them, even to their own young and tender children; these upon search are found to have dry skins and films

---

3. Frequent.

only, and be close to the flesh, keep her twenty-four hours with a diligent eye, that none of her spirits come in any visible shape to suck her; the women have seen the next day after her teats extended out to their former filling length, full of corruption, ready to burst, and leaving her alone then one quarter of an hour, and let the women go up again, and she will have them drawn by her imps close again: *Probatum est.*[4] Now for answer to their tortures in its due place.

Query seven. How can it possibly be that the Devil, being a spirit, and wants no nutriment or sustentation,[5] should desire to suck any blood? And indeed, as he is a spirit he cannot draw any such excrescences, having neither flesh nor bone, nor can he be felt, etc.

Answer. He seeks not their blood, as if he could not subsist without that nourishment, but he often repairs to them, and gets it, the more to aggravate the witch's damnation, and to put her in mind of her covenant: and as he is a spirit and prince of the air, he appears to them in any shape whatsoever, which shape is occasioned by him through joining of condensed thickened air together, and many times doth assume shapes of many creatures; but to create anything he cannot do it, it is only proper to God. But in this case of drawing out of these teats, he doth really enter into the body [of the] real, corporeal, substantial creature, and forces that creature (he working in it) to his desired ends, and useth the organs of that body to speak withal to make his compact up with the witches, be the creature cat, rat, mouse, etc.

Query eight. When these paps are fully discovered, yet that will not serve sufficiently to convict them, but they must be tortured and kept from sleep two or three nights, to distract them, and make them say anything; which is a way to tame a wild colt, or hawk, etc.

---

4. It has been proven.
5. Sustenance.

Answer. In the infancy of this discovery it was not only thought fitting, but enjoined in Essex and Suffolk by the magistrates with this intention only, because they being kept awake would be more the active to call their imps in open view the sooner to their help, which oftentimes have so happened; and never or seldom want of rest, but after they had beat their heads together in the gaol; and after this use was not allowed of by the judges and other magistrates, it was never since used, which is a year and a half since, neither were any kept from sleep by any order or direction since, but peradventure their own stubborn wills did not let them sleep, though tendered and offered to them.

Query nine. Beside that unreasonable watching, they were extraordinarily walked, till their feet were blistered, and so forced through that cruelty to confess, etc.

Answer. It was in the same beginning of this discovery, and the meaning of walking of them at the highest extent of cruelty, was only they to walk about themselves the night they were watched, only to keep them walking: and the reason was this, when they did lie or sit in a chair, if they did offer to couch down, then the watchers were only to desire them to sit up and walk about, for indeed when they be suffered so to couch, immediately come their familiars into the room and feareth the watchers, and heartneth on the witch, though contrary to the true meaning of the same instructions, diverse have been by rustical people (they hearing them confess to be witches) misused, spoiled, and abused, diverse whereof have suffered for the same, but could never be proved against this Discoverer to have a hand in it, or consent to it; and hath likewise been unused by him and others, ever since the time they were kept from sleep.

Query ten. But there hath been an abominable, inhumane, and unmerciful trial of these poor creatures, by tying them and heaving them into the water, a trial not allowable by law or conscience, and I would fain know the reasons for that.

Answer. It is not denied but many were so served as had paps, and floated, other that had none were tried with them and sunk, but mark the reasons.

1. For first the Devil's policy is great, in persuading many to come of their own accord to be tried, persuading them their marks are so close they shall not be found out, so as diverse have come ten or twelve miles to be searched of their own accord, and hanged for their labor (as one Meggs, a baker, did, who lived within seven miles of Norwich, and was hanged at Norwich Assizes for witchcraft), then when they find that the Devil tells them false they reflect on him, and he (as forty have confessed) adviseth them to be sworn, and tells them they shall sink and be cleared that way, then when they be tried that way and float, they see the Devil deceives them again, and have so laid open his treacheries.

2. It was never brought in against any of them at their trials as any evidence.

3. King James in his *Demonology* saith, it is a certain rule, for (saith he) witches deny their baptism when they covenant with the Devil, water being the sole element thereof, and therefore, saith he, when they be heaved into the water, the water refuseth to receive them into her bosom (they being such miscreants to deny their baptism) and suffers them to float, as the froth on the sea, which the water will not receive, but casts it up and down, till it comes to the earthy element the shore, and there leaves it to consume.

4. Observe these generation of witches, if they be at any time abused by being called whore, thief, etc., by any where they live, they are the readiest to cry and wring their hands, and shed tears in abundance and run with full and right sorrowful acclamations

to some justice of the peace, and with many tears make their complaints: but now behold their stupidity, nature or the elements' reflection from them, when they are accused for this horrible and damnable sin of witchcraft, they never alter or change their countenances, nor let one tear fall. This by the way, swimming (by able divines whom I reverence) is condemned for no way,[6] and therefore of late hath, and forever shall be left.

Query eleven. Oh! but if this torturing witch-catcher can by all or any of these means wring out a word or two of confession from any of these stupified, ignorant, unintelligible, poor silly creatures (though none hear it but himself), he will add and put her in fear to confess telling her, else she shall be hanged; but if she do, he will set her at liberty, and so put a word into her mouth, and make such a silly creature confess she knows not what.

Answer. He is of a better conscience, and for your better understanding of him, he doth thus uncase himself to all, and declares what confessions (though made by a witch against herself) he allows not of, and doth altogether account of no validity, or worthy of credence to be given to it, and ever did so account it, and ever likewise shall.

1. He utterly denies that confession of a witch to be of any validity, when it is drawn from her by any torture or violence whatsoever; although after watching, walking, or swimming, diverse have suffered, yet peradventure magistrates with much care and diligence did solely and fully examine them after sleep, and consideration sufficient.

2. He utterly denies that confession of a witch which is drawn from her by flattery; viz., if you will confess you shall go home, you shall not go to the gaol, nor be hanged, etc.

3. He utterly denies that confession of a witch when she con-

---

6. As wrongful.

fesseth any improbability, impossibility, as flying in the air, riding on a broom, etc.

4. He utterly denies a confession of a witch when it is interrogated to her, and words put into her mouth, to be of any force or effect: as to say to a silly (yet witch wicked enough) you have four imps have you not? She answers affirmatively, "Yes." "Did they not suck you?" "Yes," saith she. "Are not their names so, and so?" "Yes," saith she. This being all her confession after this manner, it is by him accompted nothing, and he earnestly doth desire that all magistrates and jurors would a little more than ever they did examine witnesses about the interrogated confessions.

Query twelve. If all these confessions be denied, I wonder what he will make a confession, for sure it is, all these ways have been used and took for good confessions, and many have suffered for them, and I know not what he will then make a confession.

Answer. Yes, in brief he will declare what confession of a witch is of validity and force in his judgment, to hang a witch: when a witch is first found with teats, then sequestered from her house, which is only to keep her old associates from her, and so by good counsel brought into a sad condition, by understanding of the horribleness of her sin, and the judgments threatened against her, and knowing the Devil's malice and subtle circumventions, is brought to remorse and sorrow for complying with Satan so long, and disobeying God's sacred commands, doth then desire to unfold her mind with much bitterness, and then without any of the before-mentioned hard usages or questions put to her, doth of her own accord declare what was the occasion of the Devil's appearing to her, whether ignorance, pride, anger, malice, etc., was predominant over her, she doth then declare what speech they had, what likeness he was in, what voice he had, what familiars he sent her, what number of spirits, what names they had, what shape they were in, what employment she set them about to several persons in several places (unknown to the hearer), all which mischiefs being proved to be done, at the same time she confessed to the same parties for the same cause, and all effected, is testimony enough against her for all her denial.

Query thirteen. How can any possibly believe that the Devil and the witch joining together should have such power, as the witches confess, to kill such and such a man, child, horse, cow, or the like; if we believe they can do what they will, then we derogate from God's power, who for certain limits the Devil and the witch; and I cannot believe they have any power at all.

Answer. God suffers the Devil many times to do much hurt, and the Devil doth play many times the deluder and impostor and these witches, in persuading them that they are the cause of such and such a murder wrought by him with their consents, when and indeed neither he nor they had any hand in it, as thus: We must needs argue, he is of a long standing, above six thousand years, then he must needs be the best scholar in all knowledges of arts and tongues, and to have the best skill in physic,[7] judgment in physiognomy, and knowledge of what disease is reigning or predominant in this or that man's body (and so for cattle too), by reason of his long experience. This subtle tempter knowing such a man liable to some sudden disease (as by experience I have found) as pleurisy, impostume,[8] etc., he resorts to diverse witches; if they know the man, and seek to make a difference between the witches and the party, it may be by telling them he hath threatened to have them very shortly searched and so hanged for witches, then they all consult with Satan to save themselves, and Satan stands ready prepared, with a "What will you have me do for you, my dear and nearest chil-

7. Medicine.
8. Abscess.

dren, covenanted and compacted with me in my hellish league, and sealed with your blood, my delicate firebrand-darlings." Witches: "Oh thou (they say) that at the first didst promise to save us thy servants from any of our deadly enemies' discovery, and didst promise to avenge and slay all those we pleased, that did offend us; murther that wretch suddenly who threatens the downfall of your loyal subjects." He then promiseth to effect it. Next, news is heard the party is dead, he comes to the witch, and gets a world of reverence, credence, and respect for his power and activities, when and indeed the disease kills the party, not the witch, nor the Devil (only the Devil knew that such a disease was predominant) and the witch aggravates her damnation by her familiarity and consent to the Devil, and so comes likewise in compass of the laws. This is Satan's usual imposturing and deluding, but not his constant course of proceeding, for he and the witch do mischief too much. But I would that magistrates and jurats[9] would a little examine witnesses when they hear witches confess such and such a murder, whether the party had not long time before, or at the time when the witch grew suspected, some disease or other predominant, which might cause that issue or effect of death.

Query fourteen. All that the witch-finder doth is to fleece the country of their money, and therefore rides and goes to towns to have employment, and promiseth them fair promises and it may be doth nothing for it, and possesseth many men that they have so many wizards and so many witches in their town, and so heartens them on to entertain him.

Answer. You do him a great deal of wrong in every of these particulars. For, first,

1. He never went to any town or place, but they rode, writ, or sent for him, and were (for aught he knew) glad of him.

2. He is a man that doth disclaim that ever he detected a

_____
9. Legal officers.

witch, or said, "Thou art a witch"; only after her trial by search, and their own confessions, he as others may judge.

3. Lastly, judge how he fleeceth the country, and enriches himself, by considering the vast sum he takes of every town; he demands but twenty shillings a town, and doth sometimes ride twenty miles for that, and hath no more for all his charges thither and back again (and it may be stays a week there) and find there three or four witches, or if it be but one, cheap enough, and this is the great sum he takes to maintain his company with three horses.

Judicet ullus.[10]

The End

---

10. Let anyone decide for himself.

The James Hind Pamphlets

James Hind is one of the most fascinating figures in the annals of English crime. Highwayman, prankster, and rogue, he saw himself as a seventeenth-century Robin Hood, robbing the rich in the name of the poor:

> Never did I ever wrong any poor man of the worth of a penny: but I must confess, I have (when I have been necessitated thereto) made bold with a rich bumpkin, or a lying lawyer, whose full fed fees from the rich farmer, doth too much to impoverish the poor cottage keeper.

Hind's favorite targets were what he called the "caterpillars of the commonwealth," professional men and petty officials—excisemen (tax collectors), committeemen (commissioners), long-gownmen (lawyers)—whom he hated for feeding off the common people.

Judging from the number of pamphlets about Hind (G. J. Gray names seventeen and refers to others)[1] and their favorable tone, it is evident that he was a hero to the people, if an enemy of the state.

The first of our five pamphlets, by the unidentified G. H., relates a number of incidents from Hind's salad days on the highway. A body of legends had grown up about Hind's exploits, many of which were clearly apocryphal. When asked in prison about the incidents in two well-known pamphlets, *Hind's Rambles* and *Hind's Exploits,* he declared that they were fictions. G. H. claims to have issued this pamphlet, endorsed by a dedicatory epistle ostensibly by Hind himself, to set the record straight. There is, of course, a great deal of doubt that these exploits are any less imaginary than the others that Hind objected to. However, since this book presents entertaining, popular pieces, not accurate historical documents, we include it.

1. *A General Index to Hazlitt's Handbook* (London, 1893).

The second pamphlet presents further adventures on the road, including some transvestite escapades. Again, whether these are true or not is impossible to ascertain. According to the *Dictionary of National Biography,* Hind, in Falstaffian fashion, dressed as a woman in order to escape from Colchester after it fell to Parliamentary troops during the Civil War. Perhaps this was the inspiration for the other disguise stories, or perhaps Hind's familiarity with female impersonation served him at Colchester.

The third pamphlet describes Hind's capture and imprisonment. Hind's political activities, rather than his crimes, brought about his downfall. During the Civil War, Hind remained loyal to the ill-fated Charles I, and fought with the royalist army, becoming a fugitive on its defeat. He was captured in London in 1651.

The last three selections describe Hind's imprisonment, trial, and death. In contrast to the lighthearted accounts of Hind's earlier exploits, the relation of his tearful meeting with his wife and parents in jail is quite moving. Hind was convicted of manslaughter (which he insisted he never committed) and treason. During his trial Parliament passed an act of oblivion, intended to pardon political offenders. Nevertheless, Hind was acquitted only of his criminal acts, and executed for treason.

Despite the uneven abilities of the writers, and the great range of tone as the scene shifts from the carefree days on the highway to the pathetic scene in his Newgate cell, the figure of Hind clearly emerges, undaunted and unsinkable, able to keep his sense of humor whether duping a victim, or jesting with his jailers. His pluck, especially at his death, reminds one of Ernest Hemingway's favorite "double dicho":[2] "Man can be destroyed, but not defeated."

WE HAVE BROUGHT OUR HOGS TO A
FAIR MARKET
OR
STRANGE NEWS FROM NEWGATE

Being a most pleasant and historical narrative of Captain James Hind, never before published, of his merry pranks, witty

2. A. E. Hotchner, *Papa Hemingway* (New York, 1955), p. 73: "saying which makes a statement forward or backward."

jests, unparalleled attempts, and strange designs. With his orders, instructions, and decree, to all his Royal Gang and fraternity; the appearing of a strange vision on Monday morning last, with a crown upon his head; the speech and command that were then given to Capt. Hind; and the manner how it vanished away. As also how he was enchanted by a witch at Hatfield, for the space of three years; and how she switched his horse with a white rod, and gave him a thing like a sundial, the point of which should direct him which way to take when pursued. With his speech; the old hag's charm; and the raising of the Devil in the likeness of a Lion; to the great admiration and wonder of all that shall read the same.

Imprinted at London, for George Horton, 1651.

To the Reader

Beloved Countrymen,
Whereas there hath been sundry various relations lately divulged upon the proceedings of Captain James Hind, and diverse impertinencies therein recited, which he detests against: In order whereunto at his request and desire (for general satisfaction), I have drawn up this ensuing tract; wherein is presented to thy view, his merry pranks, witty jests, unparalleled attempts, wonderful escapes, unexampled designs, never before published, and attested under his own hand; so that what hatred the effects of his feats purchased, the quaintness of them palliated; that we may well conclude,

Though Clavil's[1] fortune far more happy proved;
This lives, and yet may die, much more beloved.
                                                    G. H.

---

1. John Clavel (1603–42), a highwayman, was pardoned from his death penalty in 1627. He published a metrical autobiography in 1628.

Oyes, Oyes, Oyes

These are to certify all persons whom it may concern, that I, James Hind, do here strictly charge and require, all and every one of the Bilbo Blades,[2] lately appertaining to our Royal Gang and Fraternity, that they do not recede or flinch from their principles, nor to betray each other for the lucre of ten pounds which is the reward, and which will make them swallow a false oath as easily as one would do buttered fish; I do likewise conjure you to keep your hands from picking and stealing, and to be in charity with all men, except the caterpillars of the times, viz., long-gownmen,[3] committeemen,[4] excisemen,[5] sequestrators,[6] and other sacrilegious persons. I do likewise strictly order and command, that you keep your hands from shedding of innocent blood; that you relieve the poor, help the needy, clothe the naked, and in so doing you will eternize your fame to all ages: and make the cutting trade renowned.

Farewell,   J. Hind.

HOW HIND WAS BETRAYED BY TWO WHORES, WHO SENT TWO HIGHWAYMEN TO TAKE HIS MONEY; AND HOW HE KILLED ONE OF THEIR HORSES, AND ROBBED THE OTHER OF HIS MONEY.

Hind, being full of gold, passed away the day very merrily, and toward night, rides to an inn which stood in a private road, where it seems some highwaymen did use; after he had seen his horse carefully dressed and fed, came into the house, where were two handsome ladies by the fire; he bespoke a good supper, and invited the ladies to it; when supper was ready, he called for

---

2. Probably refers to highwaymen in general. *Bilbo* was a humorous term for the sword of a bully.

3. Lawyers.

4. City commissioners.

5. Tax officials.

6. Trustees or bailiffs having control of property on which there are claims by creditors.

wine, and made them merry; they seemed very coy to him; but knowing their humor, pulled out of his pocket a handful of gold, singing the song, "Maid, where are your hearts become, look you what here is!" After much mirth, to bed he went; he had not been long abed, but the two men came in who kept these two whores, to whom they said, that there was a gentleman in the house that had abundance of gold about him: they resolve to watch his going, and to follow him in the morning; Hind being wakeful, rose early in the morning, and was mounted before those lads were stirring: when they heard his horse prance, they looked out at a window to see him, but the thieves, seeing he had so good a horse, were like to fall out who should have him: one said, "I will have the horse, and you shall have his money"; "Nay," said the other, "I will have his horse." They quickly made themselves ready, and rode after Hind; when they had overtaken him, they asked him which way he rode; he answers them, towards Cambridge: and coming to a place where no people were nigh, one of the thieves jeers Hind, holding money in his hand, and sang, "Maid, where are your hearts become, look you what here is!" Hind seeing their intent, and knowing he was betrayed, answers them in the same tune: "Now you rogues, you are both undone, look you what here is," firing at one of them, and shot his horse in the head, which the other seeing, betook himself to flight; but Hind soon overtook him, and takes away his money, saying, "Is there but one master thief in England, and would you venture to rob him: verily, were you not of my own profession, neither of you should have lived," but seeing them ventured hard for it, "thou deservest something"; so Hind gave him his money back which he had taken from him, saying to him, "Remember what I say unto you: Disgrace not yourselves with small sums, but aim high and for great ones; for the least will bring you to the gallows, and so farewell"—O precious counsel.

HOW HIND WAS ENCHANTED BY A CUNNING WOMAN, WHO
AFTER SOME DISCOURSE SWITCHED HIM WITH A CHARMED
ROD, NOT TO BE TAKEN OR HARMED DURING THE TIME THIS
CHARM SHOULD LAST, WHICH WAS FOR THREE YEARS.

[Having robbed] the highwaymen of their money, it was his
chance [to rest. He went to] the George Inn, being then the
posthouse, where he spent the evening with some gentlemen that
were there. In the morning very early Hind called for his horse,
to be gone; being now mounted, he takes leave of the gentlemen; but as he rode along Hatfield, at the town's end, an old
woman asked an alms of him, his horse was so charitable-minded
that he presently stayed, and would go no further; "Sir," said
the old woman, "I have something to say to you, and then you
shall be gone"; Hind not liking her countenance, pulled out five
shillings and gave her, thinking she would but like a gypsy, tell
his fortune: said, "Good woman I am in haste"; "Sir," said she,
"I have stayed all this morning to speak to you; and would
you have me lose my labor?" "Speak your mind," said Hind.
Then the old woman spake as follows:

Captain Hind,
You ride and go in many dangers; wherefore by my poor skill, I
have studied a way to preserve you for the space of three years: but
that time being passed, you are no more than an ordinary man, and
a mischance may fall on you, as well as another; but if you be in
England, come to me, and I will renew the virtue of this charm again.

In saying these words, she pulled out of her bosom a box like a
sundial, and gave it Captain Hind, saying, "When you are in
any distress, open this, and which way you see the star turn
(being set at the end of a needle like a dial) ride or go that way,
and you shall escape all dangers." So she switched him with a
white rod that was in her hand, stroke[7] the horse on the buttocks,
and bid him farewell. The horse leaped forward with such

_____
7. Struck.

courage that Hind had much ado to turn him to give her thanks. The time of this charm was expired in the year 1649.

Since which time, many strange visions have appeared unto him, but especially since he came to Newgate; where, on Monday last in the morning, falling into a dream, there appeared a vision, in the likeness and portraiture of the late King Charles, with a crown upon his head, saying, "Repent, repent, and the King of Kings will have mercy on a thief."

The next morning (being Tuesday) he told one of the keepers, that he had heard of many men going to Heaven in a string; but he had been there in a dream, where he saw his master the King,[8] the noble Lord Capel;[9] but could not see Duke Hamilton.[10] The keeper replied, "Mr. Hind, was you mad to leave such a glorious place, for to come again to this dark dungeon: Truly, I am afraid you will scarce ever come there again"; and so they parted with a jest.

HOW HIND ROBBED TWO GENTLEMEN'S SERVANTS NEAR DUNSTABLE, AND CAUSED A PRESBYTERIAN MINISTER TO BE APPREHENDED FOR A HIGHWAYMAN, AND ESCAPED HIMSELF.

Hind being informed of a purchase, mounted himself upon his steed, and ranging the road, espied some gentlemen drinking at an alehouse on horseback, having sent their servants before: Hind passed by them; but riding at a good rate, quickly overtook the gentlemen's servants and soon perceived by their portmantles that there was money in them, said, "Stand, deliver your money or by the life of Pharaoh, you must forfeit your lives." The two gentlemen being too loath to dispute it with him, yielded, and resigned the portmantles, which he soon cut open, took out the money, and tying the bags together, laid them

8. Charles I, who had just been executed (January 30, 1649) by Oliver Cromwell's Commonwealth government.

9. Arthur Capel, Baron of Hadham, royalist leader, executed in 1649.

10. James Hamilton, Scottish duke, led the Scottish army into England in the royalist cause during the Civil War. He was defeated in 1648, executed in 1649.

before him, and rode full speed away. One of the servants rode to acquaint their master, who pursued Hind hard. Hind met a parson and said to him, "Sir, I am like to be robbed, you must stand to it now for your own good as well as mine. They would have this money from me, which you see. Come, sir, be of good cheer, one honest man will scare ten thieves. You shall have one of my pistols." So Hind gives the parson a pistol ready cocked and charged, and bid him fire at them that come first, "while I ride down to the next village, and raise the country people to our help." The parson having been at a wedding, and pot-valiant, rode up boldly to the gentlemen, and fired his pistol at them, but he was immediately taken prisoner, who cries out, "Spare my life, and you shall have all my money." "No, Sirra," said the gentlemen, "we will have you hanged. What, a parson and rob on the highway?" They presently hale him to the next justice of the peace, telling his worship that they were robbed almost of two hundred pounds and that this parson was one of the thieves, but the parson related the manner [how] he was drawn in by a younger brother, protesting his innocency, and that he never wronged any man of a penny. The justice laughed to see the parson of the parish apprehended for a highwayman, but passed his word for his appearance the next assizes: who, when he was brought before the bench, was cleared. But he made a vow never to fire pistols more.

HOW HIND BEING WAYLAID AT HARBOROUGH IN LEICESTER-SHIRE, RAISED THE DEVIL, IN THE LIKENESS OF A LION, AND CLEARED HIS WAY, TO THE GREAT TERROR AND AMAZEMENT OF ALL THAT BEHELD HIM.

Hind having played some notable pranks in Leicestershire, fled to the Crown Inn in Harborough, where he betook himself to a chamber, but immediately privy search was made after him, and strong guards set about the said inn, which he perceiving, came into the gallery, and inquired the cause thereof. Answer was returned that they came to make search for one who had committed a great robbery, and that there was great suspicion that he was the man. "Who, I?" said Hind. "No, I will make it manifest to the contrary. Gentlemen, I am a man sent to do wonders, and many visions have appeared, and sundry voices have I heard, saying, 'O thou great and mighty Lion, thou art decreed to range the countries to work and manifest to the people strange wonders.'" At which instant, a rampant lion appeared (visible), but immediately vanished, to the great admiration of the spectators, who peaceably departed to their several habitations, to tell the strangeness of this wonder.

> The scene's quite altered, for we plainly see
> Our English Hind is the only man. T'is he
> Doth far excell the Spanish Guzman,[11] who
> Did many brave and handsome robberies too.
> Yet is far short in that, as t'is expressed,
> For Hind could neatly rob and neatly jest.
> Tis he, the saddler's son, the butcher's boy,
> His father's grief and once his mother's joy,
> Who run from's master, and to London came
> To seek his fortune, and to get a name
> Where he not long had been, but quickly made
> Himself a member of the cutter's trade,
> And grew therein so excellent, that he
> Soon commenced master of that company:
> And this to's honor is recorded further
> The poor he robbed not, nor committed murder.

11. Probably Alonzo Perez de Guzman (1258–1309), Spanish soldier renowned for his devotion to his king. When in the battle of Tarifa the Moors threatened to kill his captive son, he declared, *"Mas pesa el rey que la sangre"* ("My king is more important than my blood"). Guzman's illegitimacy, the source of much humiliation in his youth, and his career as soldier of fortune in Africa probably gave rise to stories that he was a thief.

Coasting the country's, at the last a witch
Enchanted him, and gave his horse a switch;
Which lasted but for three years time, and then
His spell expired, and he's as other men.
And to be short, he now in Newgate lies,
In the hold a prisoner, till he's cleared or dies.
Let this suffice thee, reader, for thoul't find
The famous Guzman is our English Hind.

A PILL TO PURGE MELANCHOLY
OR
MERRY NEWS FROM NEWGATE

This is the figure, if you'll the substance see,
You must repair to Newgate, there lies he
Close prisoner, till he have answered to those crimes
Laid to his charge, since these tumultuous times.

To the courteous and ingenuous reader:
Genteels, to you I do present this book
Whose mature judgments will upon it look.
With an impartial eye, having read it, then
You'll censure't favorably, while vulgar men
Only peruse the title page, then throw't by,
Saying, it is not Hind's, but some new lie:
Let these say what they will, so it please you.
I care not if they count it false, or true;
And if these pills cure not thy melancholy,
Excuse his want of art, pass by his folly.
                    Who is ambitious of the title of
                    Your humble servant,
                         R. W.

A Pill to purge Melancholy:

Or,

MERRY NEWES

From

NEWGATE:

Wherein is set forth,

The pleasant Jests, witty Conceits, and excellent Couzenages, of Captain James Hind,
and his Associates.

How Hind, *putting on a* Bears Skin, *attempted to rob a* Committee-
man *at* Oxford *of* 200 l. *and how he had like to have been worried by a*
Mastiff Dog; *and what means he used to free himself from the fury of the*
Mastiff, *and afterwards got the money.*

How Hind *cheated an* Excise-man *of his* Mare, *which was esteemed*
one of the best in England; *and being afterwards apprehended for her at*
Newark, *how neatly he made his escape, and got the* Mare *again.*

How Hind *disguising himself in* Womens Apparel, *gul'd an old* Lawyer *in the* Temple *of* 84 l. *shewing him such a trick in the* Law, *that he*
never knew before.

How Hind *having knowledge that the* old Lawyer *had* 100 l. *more*
in his Trunk *which stood in his chamber, devised a way to get that also;*
and how he was serv'd by a Gentleman *of the* Temple, *who new chri-*
sten'd him.

With variety of other delightfull Passages, never
heretofore published by any Pen.

Let him whose mind perplexed is, with melancholy fits, Jan. 26
Buy, and read o'r this little Book, and 'twill preserve his wits.

London, Printed by *ROBERT WOOD*, 1652.

HOW HIND, DISGUISING HIMSELF IN WOMEN'S APPAREL,
GULLED AN OLD LECHEROUS LAWYER, BELONGING TO THE
TEMPLE[1], OF FOURTEEN POUNDS.

It has been a constant custom observed among the people of
this nation, to spend the time of Christmas in mirth and jollity,
using to have maskings,[2] mummings,[3] wasselings,[4] etc., at which
season our Hind (who is the main subject of the ensuing discourse) when he was in his youth, being at a private vaulting
school[5] in Chancery Lane in company of certain ladies of pleasure,
one of them laying her black bag on the table, Hind catches it
up, and puts it on his head, saying, "Do not I look like a lady?"
"I protest, so thou dost," answered one of the wenches, "and I
have seen many a lady have a worse face. Prithee go into my
chamber, and put on my gown and petticoat that lies on the
table, and go down and see if my landlady will know thee."
Hind, delighting in mirth as well as any of them, was easily
persuaded, and accoutring himself in the ladies habit, he went
downstairs with them, and there he found some of his associates,
who taking him for a gentlewoman, and knowing him to be a
stranger, they all saluted him, amongst the rest, one of them
who was called Captain Smugson, was so sweet upon him that
he could not be rid of him. Whereupon Hind desired him to
hold him excused, for he was no such kind of person as he took
him for. Smugson, thinking he meant he was no whore, but an
honest gentlewoman, replied, "What a pox do you here then?"
"Come for a wench as well as yourself, you blind owl," replied
Hind, and with that pulled off his bag and the other knew him
to be his companion, the rest laughing heartily at the mistake.
After they had caroused a while and spent their time in merry

1. The Inner and Middle Temples of the Inns of Court are British legal societies.
2. Amateur dramatic entertainments including dancing and pantomime.
3. Pantomime performances.
4. Drinking toasts.
5. Brothel.

discourse, one of the ladies desired Hind to walk forth, and take up a cully[6] (for that is the phrase they give them) and bring him thither, and they would make excellent sport with him, telling him if he went but to the Temple he should be sure to speed. He, delighting in waggery as well as the best of them, condescended, and forth he marched in the aforesaid habit, and walking between the two Temple gates, was encountered by an old rusty lawyer, one that loved his money so well, that he could not afford himself a good meal's meat, yet would give a crown or an angel to a handsome whore. This lump of corruption, meeting with our piece of mortality, cast such a lascivious look upon him that Hind presently supposed him a man fit for his purpose, and thereupon he turned back, and looked after him. Grub, seeing him look so after him, thought him to be a wench that was right for his purpose, and thereupon he came back again, saying, "Lady, I am confident I have been formerly acquainted with you," and "Sir," replied Hind, "I think I have been in your company, but I cannot call to mind where." "If it please you," saith the lawyer, "let us drink half a pint together at the Devil Tavern, and perhaps we shall call one another to mind," to which Hind consented, and so they went hand in hand to the Devil (as all lawyers and thieves will, without repentance). When they came there, the lawyer called for a whole half pint, in the drinking of which he did so beslabber Hind, and lick him under the snotgall, that he wished himself rid of him, but at last they concluded, and agreed that the lawyer should give Hind ten shillings to do the feat, but they could not agree upon the place. Hind would have had him to have gone with him to his lodging (as he called it) where his companions were, to have made sport with him there, but the lawyer thinking that further charges would arise from thence, would not consent to it, but persuaded him to

---

6. Dupe, gull.

go with him to his chamber in the Temple, into which he might privately enter, and so depart undiscovered. Hind, seeing he should be disappointed of the mirth he intended to have had with him, vowed to himself he would have his money, and so he consented to go with him thither. As soon as he was entered, he welcomed him with an old lecher's kiss, and desired him to sit upon the bed by him, which he did, and then the lawyer began to put his hand under his petticoat, but Hind desired him to forbear a while, swearing he should not touch him before he had his money. "Why think'st thou, Love, I'll be worse than my word?" quoth the lawyer, and with that puts his hand in his pocket and pulls out a good quantity of silver and about fourteen pound pieces of gold, and gave Hind his ten shillings that he had agreed for: Hind putting that into his pocket, pulled out his pistol immediately, and setting it to his breast, swore if he spake loud, or cried out, he would pistol him. So taking a gag out of his pocket (for good workmen never go without their tools) he gagged him, and bound him, and casing his pockets of his gold, in that manner left him, returning to his company, and giving them a relation of his adventure, at which the wenches laughed heartily, wishing that all lecherous curmudgeons were so served, for, said they, they have by their covetousness spoiled our trade and brought down the prices of our commodities, and swore that they could neither get money nor good ware from them, and before they would be troubled with them they would forswear their occupation.

HOW HIND, HAVING KNOWLEDGE THAT THE OLD LAWYER HAD ONE HUNDRED POUNDS IN A TRUNK THAT STOOD IN HIS CHAMBER, DEVISED A WAY TO GET THAT ALSO, AND HOW HE WAS SERVED BY A GENTLEMAN OF THE TEMPLE, WHO NEWLY CHRISTENED HIM.

Hind having left the old lecher, in manner as is before related, could not be satisfied till he was resolved what became of him after he had left him; and therefore he requested one Col. Scarface (a companion of his) to go to the Temple, and inquiring for his chamber, to pretend some business with him, and so (in all probability) he might hear how he came to be released out of that purgatory which he had left him in, at whose request Scarface went very early, and when he came to his chamber door, he found it open and the old lawyer in the same posture that Hind had left him in, who presently ungagging him, seemed very much to pity him, demanding what villain had dealt so inhumanely with him, who very faintly answered him (for he was almost spent with lying so long in that condition), that the last night there came a fellow and knocked at his chamber door, and he opening it to see who it was, he violently laid hands on him, and drawing out a pistol, threatened to shoot him if he made any noise, or stirred, so searching of his pockets, he took what money he found there, and so left him in that manner as he found him, saying moreover, that if he had not come so opportunely to have released him, he thought he should have perished. Scarface desiring to sift him further, said, "But Sir, did he take nothing from you but your money?" "No, I thank God," replied the lawyer, "nor all that neither, for I had one hundred pounds in my trunk, which by good fortune escaped his clutches." Scarface said it was a miraculous preservation and that he might rejoice that Fortune dealt so favorably with him. So breaking off that discourse (having as he supposed got sufficient intelligence from him) he began to tell him what business he came about, and laid open his case so handsomely, that the lawyer promised him he would warrant him the better of his adversary and that he would follow it for him with all diligence. So (desiring him to be careful) he gave him his fee, and departed. And coming to Hind, he told him what had happened, and what discourse had passed between them, blaming him for losing such a fortune.

"Soft," quoth Hind, "it is not lost, forbearance is no quittance; ere many days pass, I'll have that too." So after Scarface and he had steeled their noses with three or four quarts of sack, he went to a handsome whore of his acquaintance, and bestowing of a quart of wine or two upon her, fell into discourse with her, telling her, if she would be ruled by him, he would help her to a business that she should get ten pounds by. She (being willing, poor whore, to get money) promised him her assistance. Then Hind told her that she should go with him to the Temple, and that there was an old fellow there that he was confident would take her up, and carry her to his chamber, and that then she should take an opportunity to let him in, and then the business should immediately be effected with security. Having passed away the time in this and the like discourse, Hind paid the reckoning and so they departed toward the Temple, and by the way as they went he gave her further instructions what they should do. When they came to the Temple gate, Hind and his Landabrides[7] went skulking up and down thereabouts waiting for their prey; and having been an hour or two in expectation of him and seeing him not come, he began to be impatient, and walking towards his chamber, it happened that one of the gentlemen of the house having been early at the sack shop had gotten his load, and rising to empty it, happened to throw it out just upon his head, which made him almost mad, but he might be stark mad if he would, for he knew not how to help himself in that place. But being in the heat of his fury, he happened to cast his eyes up to the lawyer's chamber window, and espied a light in it, which made him confident he was about some earnest business, and feared he would hardly come out that night. Whereupon he went over to the Lion Tavern, and calling for a pint of sack, sent one of the drawers for him, bidding him to tell him that there

7. Ladylove or mistress. Lindabrides was the heroine of the English romance *Mirrour of Knighthood* (1599).

was a country gentleman at their house that must needs speak with him, giving his ningle[8] charge to keep her station, and he was confident he would not pass her, for he would leave the best friend's company he had for a whore. The drawer having delivered Hind's message to him, he laid by his writings, and had him certify the gentleman he would wait upon him immediately. As soon as the drawer was departed, the lawyer, setting his candle in the chimney corner, locked his chamber door, and followed him downstairs, but coming to the Temple gate, espied Hind's Landabrides, and not being able to pass so fair an object, stood gazing upon her, and observing her constant station, supposed she wanted a companion, and thereupon he made bold thus to salute her: "Lady, 'tis pity so excellent a creature as yourself should wait thus unattended. Wil't please you to accept of my service?" "Sir," replied she, "I wait for a gentleman, of whose fidelity I have had so good assurance, that it deserves it from me." "But trust me, Lady," said he, "he is to be blamed to make you wait so long in the cold, wil't please you to take part of a pint of wine with one who will endeavor to serve you as faithfully as he, or any man living?" She seemed something nice at the first motion, but with little persuasions she consented, and went with him. When they came to the tavern, the lawyer bid the drawer show them a room above stairs, and kindle them a couple of fagots. Hind being in a room near the bar, seeing them enter together, thought his business half done, and the wench espying of Hind gave him a wink, and went up with her frosty lover; the fire being kindled, and wine brought up, as soon as the drawer had voided the room, the lawyer began afresh to court his mistress, and to kiss and hug her close to him, proffering to feel her conundrum, etc., all which she patiently suffered; but while he was busied that way, she was not unmindful of Hind's

---

8. Darling, minion. Term rarely used to describe a female lover; normally it meant catamite.

instructions, but diving into his pocket, got his key out, which was that she looked for, which when she had gotten, she desired him to excuse her a while, for she must go down and speak with the maid. He suspecting nothing, could not deny her request; so down she went to Hind, and delivered him the key; he having what he looked for, was not long in paying his reckoning, but went immediately about his business, and coming to his chamber, unlocked the door, and breaking open his trunk secured his money for him; and locking his chamber door again, returned to the tavern. The wench having given Hind the key, returned again to the lawyer, who began again to use her as formerly, but she desired him to forbear such behavior; but if he would come to some agreement with her, she would go with him to a more private place, where they might with the more security do the feat. Thus she held him in play till Hind returned, who immediately sent up a drawer to her, to tell her, that there was a gentleman would speak with her; at which the old lawyer seemed to be discontented, but she promised him, that let it be who it would, she would but know his business, and return to him immediately, with which he was somewhat pacified. When she came to Hind, he told her he had effected his business and giving her the key, wished her to convey it into his pocket again, and so take her leave of him. So up she went again to her sweet Swatterlin,[9] who praised her for being constant to her word, and asked her who it was sent for her, bestowing many lascivious kisses upon her, while in the interim she conveyed the key again into his pocket, which done, she told him, that it was her brother had sent for her, and that she must needs go along with him. Whereat the lawyer began to fret; but upon her promise to meet him again tomorrow, he consented, and so she went to Hind, who made no staying there, but went to a more convenient place

---

9. Probably a slobberer.

to give the wench what he promised her, leaving the lawyer in a sad condition, having lost both wench and money.

HOW HIND CHEATED AN EXCISEMAN[10] OF HIS MARE, WHICH WAS ESTEEMED ONE OF THE BEST IN ENGLAND, AND BEING AFTERWARD APPREHENDED FOR IT, HOW HE MADE HIS ESCAPE, AND GOT THE MARE AGAIN.

Hind having stuffed his pockets with the lawyer's gold, the next Friday he went into Smithfield, and bought him a good gelding, and furnishing himself with a pair of pocket pistols, periwigs, and other things necessary to disguise himself, he then fell to his highway trade; and having played some exploit, riding very hard for fear of being pursued, he overtook an exciseman and his son, riding towards York, the old fellow being mounted upon as handsome a mare as ever he beheld, and as they rode together, they fell into discourse about several matters, amongst the rest, Hind inquired of the old man if that young gentleman was his son, who answered him, "Yes." "Sir," said Hind, "he is as like a brother of mine, as if one man had got them both, and still when I look upon him, me thinks I should call him so; and if you would be pleased to honor me with that title, I should be proud of it." The old man replied that he was unworthy of that name, yet if he pleased to accept of him for his father, he should be proud of so worthy a son. Thus they passed away the time in this and the like discourse, till they came to their inn, whereafter they had dismounted, and delivered their horses to the ostler, Hind goes to him, and gives him a special charge to be careful of them, and especially of his father's mare, and when he had done, he returned to his new adopted father, and told him, he had been to look after their horses, and that the ostler had promised to be very careful over them. In their familiar discourse that night at supper, they used no other terms, but *father, son,* or

10. Officer who collects excise duties (a form of taxes).

brother, insomuch that the host of the house, and all his servants, thought they had been both his own natural sons. The next morning as soon as day began to break, Hind arose, and calling for the ostler, wished him to saddle his father's mare for him, for he was to ride to a gentleman's house some two miles from that town, to speak with him about earnest business, and that he was to return again by that time the old man was stirring. The ostler quickly saddled the mare for him, and away rides Hind, and questionless he was far enough before they were up. Between six and seven of the clock, the old man and his son came out of their chamber, and making inquiry for his son Hind, the ostler told him that he caused him to saddle his mare and that he was rode out about two or three hours ago, and said he would return by that time he was stirring. Whereat the old man began to storm, protesting, he never saw him before yesterday in his life, and that he was run away with his mare, and that the master of the house should give him satisfaction. But for all his fretting, the old man was forced to pay all the reckoning, and make use of Hind's gelding to carry him home, or else he must have footed it. About a quarter of a year after, it happened that the exciseman's son being at Newark about business, Hind chanced to come riding into the same house, that he had taken up for his inn, upon his father's mare, who espying him, said, "O brother, you used my father finely, did you not?" "Friend, you are mistaken, I neither know you, nor your father." "No, Sir," said he, "but I am sure this is my father's mare." Whereupon they fell to high words, insomuch that the exciseman's son sent for the constable; and disputing the business before him, Hind asked him what paces his father's mare had? "She paced after such a manner," replied the young exciseman. "Now, Mr. Constable," said Hind, "you shall see if he is not mistaken, and I'll hold five shillings she hath no such pace." "Done," quoth the other. So Hind wished the ostler to bring forth the mare, and staked their money down in the constable's hand. Hind mounting upon her back, desired them all to take notice how she paced. He had not ridden far, but the exciseman said, "Look Gentlemen, is't not as I said?" "Ye shall see that immediately," replied Hind, and putting spurs to her, she flew like an arrow out of a bow; and away rode Hind, not so much as bidding him remember his duty to his father. Which when the company perceived, they broke forth into a great laughter, and blamed the exciseman's son for letting him to back her, saying, he might have let some other man to have ridden her. "Why," replied he, "would any man have thought he had been such a fool as to have left him money behind him. But Mr. Constable, since he is gone, we'll spend his money, and drink his health, for in my conscience he's a good fellow, but I begin to suspect he's a kind of a knave."

HOW HIND PUTTING ON A BEARSKIN, ATTEMPTED TO ROB A COMMITTEEMAN[11] AT OXFORD.

Hind having played his pranks in several places, durst not take up his constant habitation anywhere, but rode up and down the countries, still hearkening if he could hear of a good booty; and coming to the city of Oxford, it fortuned that where he took up his inn, there lay that night about half a score Worcestershire gentlemen that were going to London (it being Term[12] time) about their affairs; amongst the rest, there was a covetous committeeman, that (fearing his neighbors would tipple hard, and so he should be drawn to great expense) bespoke a shoulder of mutton for his man's supper and his own, contriving it so, that the remainder (with a flagon of beer) should serve them on the morrow for their dinner, at which the rest of his neighbors seemed to be much discontented, and mightily inveighed against him. Hind being in their company (intending to sup with them,

---

11. Commissioner.
12. The time the courts were in session and business at its peak.

in regard he was alone) seemed to excuse him, saying, "Perhaps he was short of monies." "Hang him, old usuring dog," cries one of them, "he has two hundred pounds in his portmantle, to my knowledge, which he intends to put into a scrivener's[13] hand in London, to let out a use for him." Hind hearing this, took an occasion to break off company, and causing a fire to be made in his chamber, began to study how he should compass this money. To take it from him upon the road, he perceived was impossible, he having so many in his company, and he having none of his associates about him; at last he resolved upon a way, and going to a skinner's shop, he bought a bearskin; and bringing it privately to his chamber, told the chamberlain he was not very well, and that he would go to bed; desiring him he might not be disturbed in his rest, for he had a great journey to ride tomorrow, and that he must be stirring betimes. After the chamberlain was departed, Hind began to busy himself about fitting of the bearskin for the purpose; and lacing himself in it, he waited till he saw the chamberlain carry in his supper; which as soon as he had done, and gone downstairs, our bear enters into the committeeman's chamber, which he seeing, his man and he ran out of the room downstairs, as if the Devil had been behind them. Now it fortuned, that there was a great mastiff dog belonging to the house, who seeing the chamberlain go upstairs with the meat, followed him into the committeeman's chamber, was under the table when Hind entered in that manner, who presently fell upon him, and catching hold by the nose of the bear, did so lug and tug him, that do what he could he pulled him on his back, and with tugging him, it happened that he pulled the bear's head off, and Hind's face appeared, at which sight the dog (as if he had been amazed to see it) suddenly left tugging him, and fell a barking at him; Hind being joyful he was so well rid of

13. Scriveners, scribes or clerks, often found for investors who wanted to loan money borrowers who would pay high interest for loans.

him, yet desiring to stop his mouth, took the shoulder of mutton which stood on the table, and set it down to him; which courtesy of the bear was very well accepted of by the dog, and he was quickly silenced. Hind not forgetting what he had to do, seized upon the portmantle, and, carrying it into his chamber, presently uneased himself; and taking the money out of it and putting it into his own, hung it up in the chimney, and the bearskin by it. The committeeman and his servant coming downstairs, told the man of the house (who was fudling[14] with the rest of his countrymen) that as he sat at supper, either the Devil or a bear came into his chamber, and had frighted him from it; at which the host wondered, but the countrymen laughed, and going up with him to his chamber, they neither saw bear nor Devil, but the dog, who by that time had almost filled his belly with the meat, and was a-picking of the bone, which his neighbors seeing, one of them being a notable malignant, said, "We are like to have our state well governed, when they choose those for committeemen that know not a dog from a bear." So his neighbors thinking he had been mistaken, went down and left him. The committeeman being hardly come to himself after his fright, desired his host he might have another chamber provided for him, and had his man take his things up, and carry them along with him; but when he came to gather them together, he missed his portmantle, wherein was all his money and his writings, which made him begin to threaten his host, telling him he brought it into the house, and he should bring it forth. He told him, if it had been committed to his custody, he would have made it good to him; but now there was no way for him, but to go to Lillis,[15] and inquire which of his devils was abroad that night, for certainly one of them must have it. The committeeman seeing himself thus

---

14. Tippling.
15. Reference unknown. Possibly confused allusion for Lilith, biblical demon supposed to assume the form of a beautiful woman.

jeered, sent for a constable, and caused the house to be searched, which they did; and coming to Hind's chamber, they looked about there too, but to little purpose; and seeing there was no hope of finding his portmantle, he went supperless to bed for grief, punishing his carcass for the loss of his money. In the morning Hind gets up very early, and his horse being ready saddled and bridled, he came up into his chamber, and for the committeeman's satisfaction, wrote these verses, and left them upon the table.

Those that forsake their friends to save their purse
May they be served as thou has been, or worse.
Good company hereafter ne'er decline,
But love good-fellowship; lest that the coin
For which thou carp'st, and takest so much care,
Be again taken from thee, by the bear.

THE TRUE AND PERFECT RELATION OF THE TAKING OF CAPTAIN JAMES HIND

On Sabbath day last, a discovery was made of Captain Hind's frequenting a barber's house over against Clements Church in the Strand; and the information thereof, communicated to certain gentlemen, belonging to the Right Honorable Mr. Speaker;[1] who with great privacy and care, so ordered the business, that there was not the least notice or suspicion, until such time that they came to his chamber door, who forced the same open, and immediately entered with their pistols cocked; which attempt did not a little amaze the said Hind; being so suddenly awakened out of his sleep, for not above an hour before, he had betaken himself to rest (being not very well), as he conceived in secu-

---

1. Presiding officer of the House of Commons, at this time H. Pelham.

The true and perfect

RELATION

Of the taking of Captain

JAMES HIND:

ON

Sabbath-Day laſt in the Evening at a Bar-
bers houſe in the Strand neer Clements
CHURCH.

WITH

The manner how he was diſcovered and apprehended : His Examination before the Councel
of State ; And his Confeſſion touching the
King of Scots.

ALSO,

An Order from the Councel of State concerning the ſaid Captain *Hind* ; The bringing of
him down to Newgate (yeſterday) in a Coach ;
And his Declaration and Speech delivered in priſon.

Konɡɷɓ 14

London, Printed for G. Horton, 1651.

rity; but it proved otherwise, for one who had formerly been in the King's Army, and of his intimate acquaintance, discovered him, and went along with the guard that were appointed to secure him; who no sooner was apprehended, but immediately they hasted with him to Mr. Speaker's house in Chancery Lane, where they secured him for that night.

But the next day (being Monday) by order from the Right Honorable the Council of State, the said Captain Hind was brought to Whitehall, where he was examined before a committee, and diverse questions put to him, in relation to his late engagement with Charles Stuart,[2] and whether he was the man that accompanied the Scots King, for the furtherance of his escape.

To which Hind answered, that he never saw the King since the fight at Worcester; neither did he know of his getting off the field; but he was now glad to hear that he had made so happy an escape.

After some time spent in taking of his examination, it was ordered by the committee, that he should be sent prisoner to the gatehouse, till the further pleasure of the Council of State was known therein; which accordingly done, and the said Hind was guarded from Whitehall, to the aforesaid prison: with four files of musquetiers, where he remained in safe custody that night.

The next day being Tuesday he was remanded back from thence (by special order and authority from the Council of State) to Newgate; and accordingly was brought in a coach with iron bolts on his legs; and Captain Crompton, and two other messengers belonging to the council to guard them: and about two of the clock in the afternoon they brought him to the said

---

2. Charles I, defeated, captured, and beheaded by the parliamentary forces. Hind was loyal to Charles throughout. The Puritans referred to Charles I derisively as the *Scotch King,* to show that they refused to accept his claim to rule England. Charles was the son of James I, who had been king of Scotland before taking the English throne.

place, where Captain Crompton showed the master of the prison an order of the council for his commitment, and also close imprisonment, and to let no persons whatsoever to have access to him. This order was accordingly observed: but during the time that the hole[3] was preparing for him, and the three soldiers removed to another place, that were in it before, for misdemeanors of great concernment, diverse persons frequented the place to see him, asking him several questions, to whom he returned very civil and mild answers; and among the rest, a gentleman came to him, born in the same town that he was, viz., Chipping-Norton; who took acquaintance of him, and saluting him, said, "Truly countryman I am sorry to see you in this place." He answered, that imprisonment was a comfort to him, in suffering for so good and just a cause, as adhering to the King. His countryman replied, that tomorrow (being Wednesday) he was to return home, and that if he had anything to communicate it: "I thank you Sir," said Hind, "Pray remember my love to them all, and certify them, that although I shall never see them more in this world, yet in the world to come, I hope we shall meet in glory." Then the gentleman took a glass of beer, and drank to him; which he pledged about half; and filling up his glass, said, "Come," taking the gentleman by the hand, "here is a good health to my master the King; and God bless and preserve his Majesty." But the gentleman refusing to drink the same upon such an account, moved Hind to passion, who said, "The Devil take all traitors. Had I a thousand lives, and at liberty, I would adventure them all for King Charles; and pox take all turncoats." "Forbear Sir," replied one of the keepers, "and be not in passion."

"Not in the least, I am free from it; but I could with more love and loyalty among you all: as for my own part, should I live a hundred years, I would not flinch from my principles." And

---

3. Prison cell.

then immediately (his time being short) he again spake as follows:

"Well Gentlemen, this is all that I have to say to you before I go into the dungeon, for so may I term the place where I am going to; I would have all men to be true to their trust, to stand firm and unmovable to their principles; and those that laid a foundation for their King, let them endeavor to raise it; and those that are on the contrary party, let them endeavor to demolish it. As for my part, I had not been here now, if there had not been a Judas abroad; for indeed I was betrayed by one who formerly served the King, but now he is for you"; which when he uttered, he pointed to a captain which was present, "but God forgive him."

Then one of the keepers called him from the fireside to the window, and looked about the iron shackles that were upon his legs, to see whether they were in order: "Well!" said Captain Hind, "all this I value no more than a threepence: I owe a debt to God, and a debt I must pay; blessed be His name that He hath kept me from shedding of blood unjustly, which is now a comfort to me. Neither did I ever wrong any poor man of the worth of a penny: but I must confess, I have (when I have been necessitated thereto) made bold with a rich bumpkin, or a lying lawyer, whose full-fed fees from the rich farmer, doth too much impoverish the poor cottagekeeper; And truly I could wish, that thing were as little used in England among lawyers, as the eating of swine's flesh was among the Jews." This expression caused much laughter, and many such witty jingles would he often put forth. Another gentleman standing by said, "Aye captain, but you are not brought hither for robbing, but for treason." "Treason," replied Hind, "I am not guilty of in the least." "Yes Sir, but you are, for complying with Charles Stuart, and engaging against the Commonwealth of England." "Alas Sir, it seems that it is enough then to hang me." "I am afraid you will find it so," replied the gentleman. "Well, God's will be done," said Hind,

"I value it not a threepence, to lose my life in so good a cause; and if it was to do again, I should do the like. Aye, I protest would I," laying his hand upon his breast. "Come," said the keeper, "no more of this discourse, clear the room." But a gentleman or two desired so much favor of him as to ask Mr. Hind a civil question, which was granted. So pulling two books out of his pocket, the one entitled, *Hind's Ramble,* the other, *Hind's Exploits,* asked him, whether he had ever seen them or not. He answered, "Yes." And said upon the word of a Christian, they were fictions: "But some merry pranks and revels I have played, that I deny not." Thus (Courteous Reader) have I given you the true particulars concerning Captain Hind.

Finis

THE TRIAL OF CAPTAIN JAMES HIND ON FRIDAY LAST BEFORE THE HONORABLE COURT AT THE SESSIONS IN THE OLD BAILEY.

WITH HIS EXAMINATION AND CONFESSION; HIS SPEECH TOUCHING THE KING OF SCOTS, HIS MERRY CONCEITS AND WITTY PRANKS PRESENTED TO THE JUDGES; THE MANNER OF HIS GALLANT DEPORTMENT; AN ORDER FOR HIS FURTHER TRIAL AT OXFORD; THE REASONS DEMONSTRATED; AND A CHARGE OF HIGH TREASON EXHIBITED AGAINST HIM. WITH HIS NARRATIVE AND DECLARATION TOUCHING ALL HIS PRANKS AND PROCEEDING. PUBLISHED FOR GENERAL SATISFACTION, BY HIM WHO SUBSCRIBES HIMSELF— JAMES HIND.

On Friday being the twelfth of this instant December, about two of the clock in the afternoon, Captain James Hind was ordered to be brought to the bar before the Honorable Court at the Sessions in the Old Bailey; and accordingly he was guarded from

THE
TRIAL
OF
Captain JAMES HIND on Friday laſt before the Ho

neurable Court at the Seſſions in the Old-Bayley. With his Examination and
Confeſſion ; His Speech touching the King of Scots ; His merry Conceits and
witty Pranks preſented to the Judges ; the manner of his gallant deport ; An
Order for his further Trial at *Oxford* ; the Reaſons demonſtrated ; and a Charge of
High-Treaſon exhibited againſt him. With his Narrative and Declaration touch-
ing all his Pranks and Proceeding. [*Publiſhed for general ſatisfaction, by him who ſubſcribes himſelf*
ſcribes himſelf   JAMES HIND.

JAMES   HIND.

Decemb. 15. 1651.

Newgate by the keepers; who being brought to the bar, diverse questions were proposed, which he very mildly answered. Then the recorder asked him what countryman he was, and where he was born. He replied, at the merry town of Chipping-Norton in Oxfordshire. Then it was demanded of him, whether he accompanied the Scotch King into England; and whether he was at the fight at Worcester. He answered, that he came into England with his master the King; and that he was not only at the fight at Worcester, but at Warrington also, wishing that it had been his happy fortune there to have ended his days. Then some further questions were proposed in relation to his engagement, and touching his mad pranks: to which he answered, that what he confessed before the Council of State, the like he acknowledged to that honorable court; protesting his innocency in any matter of fact or crime, since the year 1649, as appears by his ensuing declaration and narrative.

He stands indicted upon high treason by the Council of State; and thereupon the court made no further progress against him, by reason that no bill of indictment was brought in; so that he was ordered to be remanded back to the place from whence he was brought. But before his departure, this is observable: that as he passed from the bar, casting his head on one side, and looking as it were over the left shoulder, said, "These are filthy gingling spurs" (meaning his irons about his legs), "but I hope to have them exchanged ere long," which expressions caused much laughter.

As he passed up the Old Bailey toward Newgate, diverse people resorted to see him, who asked if he had received sentence; which words Mr. Hind hearing, faced to the left, and smiling, said, "No, no, good people; there's no haste to hang true folks."

Many suppose, that he will be tried by a Council of War, according to the Parliament's act on the twelfth of August: wherein all persons whatsoever that were aiding or abetting to Charles

Stuart for the carrying on of his design against the Commonwealth, are proclaimed traitors and rebels, etc. But truly I am of
this opinion, that the mercy of the Parliament will extend the
severity of justice; one thing I had almost forgot, that when he
was at the bar he deported himself with undaunted courage, yet
with a civil behavior, and smiling countenance.

The Declaration of Captain James Hind

Whereas the Heavens are doomers of men's deeds, and God
holds a balance in his hand, to reward with favor all those that
walk uprightly; and to revenge with justice all those that steer
their ways to the contrary; even so may the life of man well be
compared to the ocean seas, that for every calm hath a thousand
storms; for a little pleasure much pain; and for high desire, much
discontent: For as folly persuaded me to lead a sinful life, so at
length justice may bring me to a sorrowful end (but God re-
quires mercy in the midst thereof). Yet notwithstanding, I am
confident, the wrongs which I have committed do not cry aloud
for vengeance; but rather the mercy that I showed in all my
designs and actions, may plead an acquitment of all punishment.
However, God's will be done; for while I live my heart shall not
faint me: I sorrow not to die; neither shall I grieve at the manner of my death, though it be never so untimely. Yet could I
have but that happiness as to fight for my life, and to encounter
an enemy in the field, it would be an infinite comfort, and joy
of spirit to me. But blessed be the name of the Lord, that he hath
given me an humble spirit in these my days of tribulation, and
a heart of repentance to bewail my former course of life: for
every wrong I have done (called now to remembrance) wrings
drops of blood from my heart; although I never shed one. Neither
did I ever take the worth of a penny from a poor man; but at
what time soever I met with any such person, it was my constant

custom to ask who he was for. If he replied, "For the King," I gave him twenty shillings; but if he answered, "For the Parliament," I left him as I found him. As for any other exploits since 1649 I am guiltless of, for in the same year, May 2, I departed England (as appears by my confession to the Council at White Hat on the 10 instant, 1651) and went to the Hague; But after I had been there three days, I departed for Ireland, in the vessel that carried the King's goods, and landed at Galloway, in which kingdom I stayed three quarters of a year, part of which time I was corporal to the Marquess of Ormond's Life-Guard; And being at Youghall when that was surprised by the Parliament's forces, was there wounded in the right arm and hand with halberts.[1] After which (making a narrow escape) I went to Duncarmon, but because of the sickness, came thence to Scilly, stayed there eight months, and from thence came to the Isle of Man, stayed there 13 weeks, and went thence to Scotland, arrived at Sterling, where I sent a letter to his Majesty, acquainting his Highness of my arrival, and represented my service, etc. Which was favorably accepted of; for no sooner had the King notice of my coming, but immediately I had admittance into his chamber, and kissed his hand; and after some discourse, his Majesty commended me to the Duke of Buckingham then present, to ride in his troop because his Life-Guard was full. I came to England with the said troop, was in the engagement at Warrington, also at Worcester, where I kept the field, till the King was fled, and in the evening, the gates being full of flying persons, I leapt over the wall on foot by myself only, traveled the country, and lay three days under bushes and hedges, because of the soldiery, till I came to Sir John Packington's woods, where I lay five days; and afterward came on foot to London, by the name of James Brown, lodged five weeks in London, and was taken 9 November at Denzy's the barber near Dunstan's Church in Fleet Street.

---

1. Weapon—combination between spear and battle-ax.

This is all that was declared and confessed by him, who remains captivated in close prison in the Gaol of Newgate.

James Hind

On the 13 of this instant it was declared that the said Mr. Hind's further trial was to be adjourned from the Old Bailey, to the city of Oxford, and in order thereunto, to receive a trial in the Castle Hall, to the end, that he may receive condign punishment in the same county where first he committed his fact and crimes, and that all those who have suffered by him may the better give in evidence, and prosecute the business against him. As for any bills of indictment, or witnesses to prove the allegations, nothing can be made apparent, neither are any come in. And this is observable, that upon his first coming before the court, he was asked, whether his name was James Hind: "Yes, if it shall please you, my name is honest and loyal James Hind; in testimony whereof, my right hand, having lost part of the use thereof, bears me testimony; and so God bless all true subjects."

FROM THE ENGLISH GUZMAN OR THE HISTORY OF THAT UNPARALLELED THIEF, JAMES HIND

THE DISCOURSE BETWEEN HIS FATHER, HIS WIFE, AND HIMSELF, IN NEWGATE, THE 28 OF NOVEMBER.

Hind's father, hearing of his son's misfortune, came to London, and brought his son's wife with him: but there being such strict orders that one should go to him, his father and his wife could not be admitted to see him, but lodging at one of the keeper's houses, the next day was brought to him. The good old man with tears in his eyes began to behold his son, who was

THE
Englifh Gufman;
OR THE
HISTORY
Of that Unparallel'd Thief
JAMES HIND.

Wherein is Related

I. His Education and manner of Life; alfo a full Relation of all the feverall Robberies, madd Pranks, and handfom Jefts done by Him.

II. How at HATFIELD he was Enchanted by a

WITCH

For three years fpace; and how She *Switch'd* His Horfe with a white *Rod*, and gave him a thing like a Sun-dial, the Point of which fhould direct him which way to take when perfued.

AND

III. His Apprehenfion, Examination at the Councel of State. Commitment to the *Gatehoufe*, and from thence to *Newgate*, His Arraignment at the *Old Baily* ; And the difcourfe betwixt his Father, his Wife and Himfelf in *Newgate*.

With feveral Cuts to Illuftrate the Matter.

Written by G. F. *Gan* 10

London Printed by *T. N.* for *George Latham* Junior, and are to be fold at the Bifhops-Head, in Paul's Church-Yard, 1652.

Herenow thou feeſt, me as a *Butchers* Boy,
And ſporting with a *Dog* in Merriment :ꞏ
Heƥeafter thou wilt read the *Tricks* I play,
Which may afford Thee *pleaſure* and *content.*
For there's no *Robb'ry* yet I ere did doe,
But doth contain at leaſt a *Jeſt,* or two:

kneeling at his father's feet, but was scarce able to rise for the
weight of irons that was on his legs, but being helped by his
father, arose, and went to his wife, who stood wringing her
hands, to see her husband in that misery. She, taking him about

the neck, wept to see him, kissing him a thousand times; after they had discoursed a while his father speaks as follows:

"Son, I hope it is not too late to give you counsel: but I wish to God you had taken my former counsel, and then I might not have come here to see you. You do not think how much it goes to my heart, and all your friends, to think what will become of you."

"Father, I hope the Lord will look upon a sinner that truly repents, and is sorry from the bottom of his heart for his offenses: and I make no doubt but that the State will have as much mercy on me, as ever the late king had on Clavil,[1] who was far more in danger than I am now."

"Son, son, be not too confident; for when a ship is cast away by bulging[2] on rocks that are near the shore, those that can swim may be saved, but those that cannot must take their fortune. Even so it is with you, for friends that should stir in your business, I have none; and that which should do you most good, doeth you the most injury. I shall desire you upon my blessing to bridle your speech, and let not envy be in your heart to any one: let not this counsel be like water spilt upon the ground, but make use of it for the best."

"Father, I shall by the help of God follow your advice; and I desire the world not to look back on my actions, but forward, and they shall find me an altered man."

"Husband, I would once more you were at liberty, that I might see this change, which would make both soul and body happy."

The keeper, having occasion to be gone, desired them to depart for that time: so taking their leave of him, they went to their lodging.

---

1. John Clavel, highwayman pardoned by Charles I.
2. Striking so as to damage to bilge.

No Jest like a true Jest.
Being a Compendious
RECORD
OF THE
Merry Life and mad Exploits
OF CAPT.
JAMES HIND,
The Great Robber of England.
TOGETHER WITH
The Close of all at *Worcester*, where he
was drawn, hanged, and quartered, for
High-Treason, against the Common-
wealth, *Sept.* 24, 1652.

FROM NO JEST LIKE A TRUE JEST. BEING A COM-
PENDIOUS RECORD OF THE MERRY LIFE AND
MAD EXPLOITS OF CAPT. JAMES HIND, THE
GREAT ROBBER OF ENGLAND, TOGETHER WITH
THE CLOSE OF ALL AT WORCESTER, WHERE HE
WAS DRAWN, HANGED, AND QUARTERED, FOR
HIGH TREASON, AGAINST THE COMMON-
WEALTH, SEPTEMBER 24, 1652.

THE CONCLUSION, AND HIND'S FAREWELL AT WORCESTER

On Friday the thirteenth of December, 1651, Captain Hind
was brought to the Sessions House in the Old Bailey, where diverse questions were asked, concerning his life and conversation.
He answered in the same manner as he had done before the
Council of State, protesting his innocency in any crime, since the
year 1649, within any of the parliamentary dominions. So he
was dismissed from that place, and on Monday the first of March,
1652, he was carried in a coach from Newgate to Reading in
Berkshire, where he was arraigned on the Wednesday following,
before Judge Wetherton, was found guilty of manslaughter, and
condemned to die; but the next morning the act of oblivion[1]
being sent, he was acquitted of all former offenses, only the indictment of high treason against the State, for which he was
carried to Worcester, and there drawn, hanged, and quartered,
on Friday, the twenty-fourth of September, 1652.

> Thus Fate the great derider did deride;
> Who lived by robbery, yet for treason died.

Finis

---

1. An act of oblivion grants general pardon for political offenses. Here, strangely,
Hind is pardoned his nonpolitical crimes, and executed for treason.

The Ranters Ranting

The English Renaissance was a time of religious intolerance. Everyone believed that there was one true faith, but there was a great deal of disagreement about which one it was. Henry VIII put Catholics to death for refusing to reform their religion. When the Catholics returned to power with Mary, they burned Protestants at the stake, as Foxe's *Book of Martyrs* records in grisly detail. With the accession of Elizabeth, the persecution of Catholics began again.

In the early decades of the seventeenth century, the Puritans found conditions so harsh that many emigrated to the terrifying wilderness of America. And when the Puritans came to power under Cromwell, they themselves were far from tolerant of religious dissent, as this pamphlet on the Ranters shows.

The Ranters were a Protestant sect during the time of the Commonwealth. Their central doctrine was pantheistic: they believed that God exists in every creature. All Ranters rejected the established Church and Scripture; many also rejected belief in immortality, and the idea of a personal God.

The Ranters were strongly antinomian—that is, they believed that Christians are freed from moral law by the dispensation of grace. Although most of what is written about them is heavily biased one way or another, they seem to have been religious fanatics rather than dissipates. Their fellow Britons, however, refused to believe that a group that denied the authority of moral law, and did not believe in hellfire, could possibly be anything but dissolute, wild-eyed sinners.

The movement became fairly widespread in England during the 1640s and 50s before it was suppressed by Parliament. The pamphlet seems to be a pure example of bigotry and slander. In all probability the behavior of the Ranters is invented, and their beliefs caricatured.

142

We print the pamphlet not to give information about the Ranters, but rather to reveal seventeenth-century attitudes toward religious dissent.

It is not surprising that the Ranters were despised in their own time; it is surprising to find that prejudice against them lingered into the twentieth century. The eleventh edition of the *Encyclopaedia Britannica*, published in 1910, describes the Ranters as the "dregs of the Seeker movement," and says of them, "How far the accusation of lewdness brought against them is just as hard to say, but they seem to have been a serious peril to the nation." Today, just what the peril was is hard to say.

THE RANTERS RANTING

Behold, ye Despisers,
Wonder and Perish.

Upon the first day of November 1650 (toward evening) came one Shakespeare (that called himself a warrener),[1] one John Collins, a glover, one Wyberton, and four others to the house[2] of one Middleton, at the David and Harp in Moor Lane, in the parish of Giles Cripplegate, London, where some of them being known, they were soon admitted into the best room in the house, and it grew something late in the evening, when the street was void of noises, and sober men prepared to go to bed, these people were heard to sing blasphemous songs in the tune of David's Psalms, and many uncivil words and actions were perceived and heard to pass amongst them; which put it into hearts of some of the neighbors to acquaint the constable therewith; who being as desirous to suppress disorders, as willing to bring such wicked persons to condign punishment, he took some others with him to apprehend them; but to make the fuller discovery of this wicked pack, one that had some acquaintance with an active Ranter, went alone to the door where this wicked company were, and enquired of John Collins that opened it, whether such a one were

---

1. Officer employed to watch over game in a park or preserve.
2. Public house, or bar. The David and Harp refers to the picture on his sign.

The Ranters Ranting :

W I T H

The apprehending, examinations, and confession of *Iohn Collins,*
I, *Shakespear, Tho. Wiberton,* and five more which are to answer
the next Sessions. And severall songs or catches, which were sung
at their meetings. Also their several kinds of mirth, and dancing.
Their blasphemous opinions. Their belief concerning heaven and
hell. And the reason why one of the same opinion cut off the
heads of his own mother and brother. Set forth for the further
discovery of this ungodly crew.

LONDON
Printed by *B. Allop,* 165?

not amongst them? Who replied, he was not there yet, but was
expected; asking him if he was of his acquaintance: to which the
party answered, that he was: then Collins took him about the
neck, and kissed him, saying, "Welcome fellow creature." With

this the party came into the room, where the like ceremony was offered by the rest (some women being also amongst them). Presently after, one of the men let his breeches slip down in the middle of the room, and another ran and kissed his buttock, and called to the rest to come and kiss their God. And after the passing away of a little more time in blasphemous words and uncivil behavior, a joint of incat[3] and some other things were brought and set upon the table, about which they flocked like brute beasts, without any order, or sign of reverence; but on the contrary one of them laid hold on the meat, and tearing it to pieces like a dog, both for himself and the rest of his fellow creatures, in a beastly manner he let a great fart, and as it gave report, he uttered these words, "Let every thing that hath breath praise the Lord."

In the middle of which profane and wicked words and behavior, came in the constable and apprehended them, who thinking them to be given over to commit all manner of wickedness, thought good to search their pockets, for fear they might have some dangerous weapons about them to do mischief, and in searching them, he found two written papers stuffed with very blasphemous matter, which are not fit to be made public, especially until such time as they have received their trial. When this was done the constable brought them downstairs into another room, and himself and others reproved them for their wickedness, in the midst of which reproof, one of them that were taken took a candle and made as though he did seek for something that he had lost, and being asked what he sought for, in a jeering and disdainful manner he answered that he sought for his sins but there were none, and that which they thought so great unto him, was so small, he could not see it, by which it appears that they hold forth an opinion, that sin is no sin, for which opinion an officer of the army was lately cashiered, and

---

3. Word unknown.

his sword broken over his head, at the head of the regiment. But to return to that which I was relating before, the constable finding them desperately incorrigible and hardened in their iniquity, carried the said Collins, Shakespeare, and five others to the Counter[4] (who had been accompanied by Mrs. Middleton herself, had she not privately made an escape).

The next morning they were brought before Sir John Welaston, and charged with the matters before recited; as also that they had sung vile and filthy songs to the tune of Psalms, and uttered many oaths (or asseverations of oaths) and execrations: some of which were, "Ram me, Dam me, etc.," and it being demanded of one of them what they meant by these words, he said by the word *ram,* they meant *God;* and many other things of this nature were confessed by them: whereupon Sir John sent them to Bridewell,[5] where for a time they beat hemp; and are bound over to answer for their offenses, according to the law the next sessions.

Having given you the true relation of this meeting, with the manner of their discovery, and some passages concerning their examinations, I shall proceed to some other instances to show the vanity of this mad crew (of which there be too many) for all pleasures which are not reduced to honesty and necessity are reproachful and evil, and especially those two of touching and tasting, do draw men most to offend in vice and uncleanness; and forasmuch as all occasions and opportunities, whereby the people are trained and drawn away to live dishonestly, shamelessly, wickedly, and intemperately are to be shunned and avoided, take in the next place some particulars of another meeting which they had near Thames Street (not long before the act was made against blasphemy, and another act for whoredom, etc.). As soon as they came together they coupled men and women, choosing their mates, and when they had fitted themselves in

4. A London prison.
5. A London prison.

that kind, there comes into the room a man with a pottle of sack, and a glass in his hand uttering these words, viz., "Where doth God want any wine?" To which presently answered one that had his minion on his knee, "Here, here," at which words the glass of sack was given him, and he drank to his fellow creature (as he called her) and so it went round. After this they fell to singing filthy songs and catches which are not fit to be published, yet, for satisfaction sake, I shall give one of their songs to the first scene, when they began to act upon the Devil's stage, what every one pleased, according to the fullness of wickedness in his own heart, which was taken at the window, and in truth, is the least offensive of any I have heard, otherwise I should have had more modesty than to have made it public.

The song that was sung at the first meeting together of a company of Ranters:

> This is the merry meeting of
>   The creatures set apart
> To exercise their liberty,
>   And teach the Mother's art.
> If Adam were deceived by Eve,
>   It was because he knew
> Not how to exercise the gifts
>   Which nature did indue.[6]
> The slavish terror that men have,
>   And thoughts of hell to fear
> Is unto us a laughing stock,
>   We give to it no ear.
> Some men another world do prize
>   Of which they have no measure,
> Let us make merry, sing, and dance,
>   There is no heaven to pleasure,

6. Endow.

Which we enjoy with sweet content.
A short life, and a merry,
Is all the heaven that we expect,
Let's drink off our canary.[7]
The fellow creature which sits next
Is more delight to me
Then any that I else can find;
For that she's always free.
Yet whilst I speak of loving one,
Let no mistaking come;
For we that know our liberty,
In loving all love none.
But for to satisfy our lust
And beastly appetite,
Not caring what we do or say,
So we may take delight.
Then let us rant it to the fill
And let our love too range,
For it hath wings, and they are freest
That in their loves do change.

This song being ended, they went to reveling till ten of the clock the next day, by which time, they having satisfied themselves with chamber exercise, they fetcht a walk towards Smithfield, and went into Charterhouse Lane, where they had a lesson played on the organs, danced mixed dances, and had an antic mask;[8] and during the time of the masking, the music that played was the treble-viol, the hand-symbol, and tongs. After this the organs went anew, to the tune of a psalm. After this, some of the creatures went into rooms apart to milk and fodder; and others (whose chiefest pleasure was in drinking) sung this catch following,

---

7. A sweet white wine.
8. Short musical play with grotesque costumes and a great deal of dancing.

A Drinking Song

Drink today and drown all sorrow,
You shall perhaps not do't tomorrow;
Best while you have it use your breath,
There is no drinking after death.
Wine works the heart up, wakes the wit,
There is no cure 'gainst age, but it;
It helps the headache, cough, and tissick,
And is for all defenses physic.
Then let us swill, boys, for our health;
Who drinks well, loves the Commonwealth:
And he that will to bed go sober,
Falls with the leaf still in October.

Unto this I shall add another, somewhat pertinent to the business, viz.: A gentleman of quality (as I am credibly informed) meeting with a gentlewoman of his acquaintance, after a salutation, "How do you," and a little familiar discourse, he told her he was indifferent well in health, but wanted a stomach, whereupon she replied that if he pleased to come to her lodging the next day, she doubted not but she should find something to which he had an appetite, for which courteous invitation, in a civil manner he returned thanks, and promised a visit the next day about eleven of the clock: at which time according to appointment he made good his promise; and being invited up into her chamber, he found her in her night array; and after the first greeting was over, she asked him how he found his stomach? He replied, that it was as when he left her the day before; she then said, that she hoped it would soon be regained: and on the sudden, instead of putting on her day apparel, disrobed herself of what she had on, and appearing in nothing but her smock, asked him how he liked her, and whether his stomach would not come to him? To which he replied, that he understood not her meaning; but he hoped to have a stomach to his victuals when it was before him: then she said, I will try that presently; and immediately presented herself to him naked, saying, "Fellow creature, what sayest thou to a plump leg of mutton," striking her hand upon her thigh, "with the cates that are now in thy view?" which strange carriage of hers did so appal this virtuous gentleman, that he (in blushing wise) departed, wondering at the shameless, uncivil carriage of her, of whom he had better confidence; which may be read and commended for a badge of his virtue and chastity, and characterize the deserved infamy of the lascivious behavior of her that was empty of all goodness, and discover her to be a true proselyte of Cop[9] and Claxton[10] and the rest of that infernal gang which have been the dispensers of a diabolical opinion that there is neither heaven nor hell, for otherwise she could not be so audacious.

Having named Cop, I cannot let it pass without a word or two of what he is; he is one that not long since ashamed the pulpit in a noted church in London, and in a most wicked manner blasphemed and cursed, for an hour together saying, "A pox of God; take all your prayers hearing, reading, fasting, etc." And being charged before he came down with uttering blasphemy, he said that he would answer what he had done, and for this and other things of like nature laid to his charge, he is now in Newgate,[11] and to discover what might be said of him alone, would fill many sheets of paper; at this time I have promised brevity; therefore I shall only add to that in the pulpit, a passage of his on an alehouse bench, which is this: when he had drunk very hard and the woman of the house, to avoid disorder, desired him and his company to depart the house, he said, "God damn me,

9. Abiezer Coppe (1619–72), Baptist preacher, member of the Ranters. His tract "Fiery Flying Roll" had just been burned as blasphemous by order of Parliament.

10. Lawrence Claxton (1615–67), controversial Antinomian sectary, whose tract "Single Eye of Light" had just been burned by order of Parliament.

11. A London prison.

and thou needst not fear. The Devil confound me, thou art in heaven. By God's blood and wounds, thou art saved, etc.," which put the woman into such a fright to hear his curses and blasphemies, that she trembled and quaked some hours after.

I thought to have given you many other particulars, but I hope these are sufficient to satisfy all good people concerning the wicked practices and blasphemous opinions of this generation which have too long increased, and from what hath been said by way of discovery, take warning and avoid their company which may prove dangerous to the body as well as to the soul: for I am able to justify that one Evan ap Beven, born of good parentage near Bishops-Castle in the County of Salop,[12] was for many years a constant hearer of the word, yet afterward fell into strange opinions and would admit of no sacrament, no baptism, no duty, no obedience, no Devil, no hell, etc. In a short time after his fall into these grand errors (the Devil growing strong with him) that for no other cause but that they were conscientious and finding an opportunity, he cut off the heads of his own mother and brother, for which he was hanged in chains near Shrewsbury.

Finis

---

12. Shropshire.

News from the Tower Hill

From what we can tell from contemporary records and literature, the world's oldest profession did a thriving business in Elizabethan England, particularly in London and its notorious suburbs. The most interesting thing about the ballad "News From Tower Hill" is the sexist attitude of the author, "M.P." Although we do not know his name, there can be no doubt about his gender: he sees prostitution as strictly a female problem—if loose women did not set out to entice innocent young men, there would be no fornication. It does not seem to occur to him that if there were no customers, there would be no whores.

The notion that women are the root of evil was a strongly ingrained one in medieval and Renaissance Europe. Many of the Church Fathers—most notably Tertullian and St. Jerome (see the "Wife of Bath's Tale" for the full list)—made misogyny a powerful strain in Christian thought. Not everyone shared this outlook, however: Shakespeare seemed to realize that prostitution operates on a supply and demand basis. In *Measure for Measure,* when Escalus tells Pompey that prostitution shall be no longer tolerated in Vienna, Pompey asks, "Does your worship mean to geld and splay all the youth of the City?" Escalus answers, "No," and Pompey replies, "Truly, sir, in my poor opinion, they will to't then."

NEWS FROM THE TOWER HILL
or
A gentle warning to Peg and Kate,
To walk no more abroad so late

To the tune of "The North Country Lass"

The second part,   To the same tune.

So out of doores be tript,
and made a fine crouse,
The Lasses sild their Wine did fill
as twas their former vse.

But when they long had stayd,
and the Lad came no more,
The Vintner came of them to clayme
money to cleere the score.

They sayd they had no money,
to pay for what was drawne,
Their Aprons they vntill next day
and kniffes would leaue in pawne.

The Vintner would haue none,
but sware he would be payd
Ere then did passe, or else was
in prison they must be stayd.

All night they tarryed there,
ith morning Peg did send
To her Mother deare, who came to her
as did become a friend.

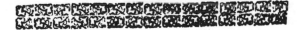

Her Husband came with her,
and he did passe his worde,
At a certaine day the shot to pay
which they that night had consum'd.

And so they were dismist,
well serued I protest:
If all base whores might pay such scores
then men might passe in rest.

The yongman I commend,
and wish that others would
Him imitate, then Peg and Kate
would be no more so bold.

It is a great abuse,
in London at this day,
Now in the streete many nightly walk
such wenches on the way.

Which causeth many a man,
that would goe home in quiet,
Vpon such queans to spend his meanes,
in slubbinesse and ryot.

London Printed for E. B.   Finis. M P.

Newes from the Tower-hill:
OR,
A gentle warning to *Peg* and *Kate*,
To walke no more abroad so late.

To the tune of the North countrey Lasse.

A Pretty iest Ile tell,
  which was perform'd of late,
Let Lasses all in generall,
  be warned by Peg and Kate.

These Lasses both doe dwell,
  neere Algate at this day,
A vse they had ith night to gad,
  abroad as I heard say.

To meete with some young men
  on them to shew affection,
Which vse they still on Tower-hill
  did keepe by one direction.

But now giue heede a while,
  and marke how they were serued,
Would all were so that thus doe goe
  then men might be preserued.

From these deluding bayts,
  which by the way doe catch them
Let all young men be carefull then,
  and marke how one did match them.

As they walkt forth one night,
  as t'was their custome still,
A youngman kind did chance to finde
  them vpon Tower-hill.

And finding them so free,
  and easie to goe bettime,
He got them both they were not loth
  with him to Greenewich Towne.

A payre of Oares he tooke,
  and thither went in hast,
While all that night they had delight,
  but marke what after past.

He brought them vp next day,
  and at the Posterne gate,
Into the shipe they all did shipe,
  at night when it was late.

Where they to supper had
  all dainties they could wish,
Young Rabbets fry'd they bone youths
  and rost Eeles in a dish.

And Lambe they had beside,
  with Wine and Sugar fine,
And musicke sweet which made the feast
  to make them pay say more.

At last the reckoning came
  to two and twentie shilling,
The Lad he as wise and did deuise
  to make them pay say billing.

A pretty jest I'll tell,
    which was performed of late.
Let lasses all in general
    be warned, Peg and Kate.

These lasses both do dwell
    near Algate at this day,
A use they had i'th night to gad
    abroad as I heard say.

To meet with some young men
    on them to shew affection,
Which use they still on Tower Hill
    did keep by due direction.

But now give heed a while,
    and mark how they were served,
Would all were so that thus do go
    then men might be preserved.

From these deluding baits,
    which by the way do catch them,
Let all young men be careful then,
    and mark how one did match them.

As they walked forth one night,
    as twas their custom still,
A young man kind did chance to find
    them upon Tower Hill.

And finding them so free,
    and easy to go down,
He got them both, they were not loath,
    with him to Greenwich Town.

A pair of dares[1] he took,
    and thither went in haste,
While all that night they had delight,
    but mark what after past.

He brought them up next day,
    and at the postern[2] gate,
Into the Ship[3] they all did skip,
    at night when it was late.

Where they to supper had
    all dainties they could wish,
Young rabbits fried they bade provide
    and roast beef in a dish.

And lamb they had beside,
    with wine and sugar store,[4]
And music sweet which made the street
    to muse how they did roar.

At last the reckoning came
    to two and twenty shilling,
The lad was wise and did devise
    to make them pay for billing.[5]

The second part, to the same tune:

So out of doors he crept,
    and made a fine excuse,

---

1. Portions.
2. Back, rear.
3. A tavern.
4. In plenty.
5. Caressing.

The lasses still their wine did fill
    as 'twas their former use.

But when they long had stayed,
    and the lad came no more,
The vintner came of them to claim
    money to clear the score.

They said they had no money
    to pay for what was drawn,
Their aprons they until next day
    and ruffs would leave in pawn.

The vintner would have none,
    but swore he would be paid
Ere they did pass, or else alas
    in prison they must be stayed.

All night they tarried there,
    in morning Peg did send
To her mother dear, who came to her
    as did become a friend.

Her husband came with her,
    and he did pass his word,
At a certain day the shot[6] to pay
    which they that night had scored.[7]

And so they were dismissed,
    well served I protest:

6. Tab.
7. Run up.

If all base whores might pay such scores
Then men might pass in rest.

The young man I commend,
   and wish that others would
Him imitate, then Peg and Kate
   would no more be so bold.

It is a great abuse,
   in London at this day,
Now in the street many nightly meet
   such wenches on the way.

Which causeth many a man,
   that would go home in quiet,
Upon such queans[8] to spend his means,
   in filthiness and riot.

M. P.

London
Printed for E. B.

---

8. **Whores.**

Look on Me London

Look on Me London deals with cony-catching, the art of separating well-heeled fools from their money. (Cony literally meant rabbit, figuratively, dupe.) Cony-catching pamphlets, describing in great detail the practices of London crooks and swindlers, were very popular in Elizabethan times, starting with John Awdeley's *The Fraternity of Vagabonds* (1561). The best of the cony-catching pamphleteers was playwright Robert Greene, the Cambridge graduate who lived in the London underworld. Greene's *A Notable Discovery of Cozenage Now Daily Practiced by Sundry Lewd Persons Called Cony-Catchers and Crossbiters*, and a *Second* and *Third Part of Cony-Catching*, are among the best of their type.

Our pamphlet, *Look on Me London*, is a countrydweller's advice to his son, who is going to London. Since the first urbanites gathered in cities there has been antipathy between town and country, but there was an added element of hostility in Elizabethan times because of friction between the urban middle classes and the rural gentry. Throughout the sixteenth century, as capitalism replaced the old feudal economic order, the humble artisans of the Middle Ages became the prosperous tradesmen of the Renaissance. Inflation steadily eroded the value of land, the basis of the aristocracy's wealth, while it enriched the merchants, so that the bourgeois began to replace the gentry as the wealthiest class in England. The citizens did what they could through marriage and acquisition of land to add status to their wealth, and this caused a great deal of resentment on the part of the gentry.

During the sixteenth century, London became not only a center of commerce, but of culture and entertainment as well, and as a result, young gentlemen were eager to sample the pleasures of the city. What with their dissolute tastes and the numbers of swindlers and merchants ready to fleece them, many lost their patrimonies and were completely ruined in very little time. After a gentleman squandered what money he brought with him on whores, cards, or dice, he often took a loan from a merchant (there were no banks then), giving his land as security. Eventually the dupe lost his land, or went to jail for debt.

Although the gentlemen conies are sympathetic to a degree in that the merchants and sharpers often lay for them and cheated them, to a large extent they brought their troubles on themselves because of their fondness for gambling, drinking, and prostitution. Furthermore, their attitude toward the tradesmen was one of utter disdain, and they often felt little or no obligation to pay for what they purchased. Their attitude seemed to be that the aristocracy should be well outfitted, that tradesmen existed for that purpose, and that the privilege of equipping a gentleman ought to be payment enough for a merchant. Sir John Falstaff's contempt for Master Dombledon, his tailor, and his refusal either to give security or to pay in advance for his slops, was not an unusual attitude for a knight in Shakespeare's time.

The conflict between the gentlemen and the merchants was the subject of a number of Jacobean comedies, the best among them Thomas Middleton's "city comedies," *Michaelmas Term* and *A Trick to Catch the Old One*. These plays pit young, attractive gentlemen against foul, old, grasping citizens. Our pamphlet sides with the gentlemen, placing the blame for the "moral envy between the two estates" on "cruel usage of covetous merchants in former ages."

LOOKE ON ME LONDON

To the young men of London, as well gentlemen as others:

I am persuaded, that in this dedication, I do salute the most part of all the young gentlemen of England, in that they either dwell, or have been in this worthy city of London, where they have seen many wanton alectives[1] to unthriftiness, which like to enchanting adamant[2] rocks, draws gold and silver as fast as iron and steel.

---

1. Enticements.
2. Imaginary mineral of magnetic properties.

Looke on me London:

I am an Honeſt Engliſh-man, ripping vp the Bowels of Miſchiefe, *lurking in thy Sub-vrbs and Precinƈts,*

TAKE HEED

The Hangmans Halter, and the Beadles Whip,
will make the Foole dance, and the Knaue to skip.

LONDON,
Printed by *N. O.* for *Thomas Archer,* and are to bee
ſold at his ſhop in Popes-head Palace neere
the Royall Exchange. **1 6 1 3.**

Therefore (young men) you must be armed with more experience than the capacity of young years, or else, assure yourselves, repentance will unloose your fetters. For truly, I cannot see how young men of the best education can scape untangled, when vice is so conversant with elder years. O how happy were it for your posterity if all dicing houses and alleys of gaming were suppressed in and about this city. From which, if you cannot be drawn, this little book will guide you safe, and give you fair warnings of many of your companions' falls. I beseech you be advised, and learn to shun these mischiefs by other men's harms, that the reward of this my writing may prove fortunate, and myself happy to see you thrive and flourish.

I dedicate this book to the honorable magistrate, to whom appertaineth the correction of evil livers, your worst enemies; I mean the sucking shifters now secretly lurking in the circuits of this famous city, of whom his good honor, I hope, will ease you, and make you prosperous by the reformation. So leaving to trouble you with a tedious induction, I end at this time, but in no time will leave to be

Your well-wishing friend.

R. I.

A Countryman's Counsel

GIVEN TO HIS SON AT HIS GOING UP TO DWELL AT LONDON, BEING A TRUE TOUCHSTONE FOR THIS AGE, FOUND OUT BY TIME AND EXPERIENCE.

London, where thou intendest to go (son William) and set up thy life's resting place, is at this day (as thou knowest) the capital city of our country, and the paragon of Christendom, a place of much honor and reputation, as well in respect of reverent government, as sumptuous building and riches. London (I say) is the strength and ornament of this well-governed land, unto which place every gentleman, and almost yeoman of ability, sendeth the ripest witted of his children, either to study the common laws of England, or become merchants to enrich their country, wherein the love of a father to his son is discharged, and the duty of a friend to his country performed.

But yet this admonition from me thy father: In this good city are many alectives to unthriftiness, by which means, where the father hath been at charge to make his son a lawyer, to do his country service, or a merchant or a tradesman and to be a good member to this flourishing city, his aforesaid son (for want of government) many times spent his whole substance to the utter undoing of his posterity, and the great shame of his kindred. Therefore, take heed my son; one scabbed sheep infecteth a whole flock and one wasteful prodigal makes a swarm of unthrifts: of which many there be now, that live in, and about the city of London, that would quickly seize upon thee, and such fond young man as thou art, and by their lewd conditions draw thee from study, or from thy other business, and bring thee acquainted with their wicked consorts and companions; and where must it be but in ordinaries,[3] dicing houses, bowling alleys, brothel houses, and such like, where their bravery, reveling, and merry company is able to bring a staid man into their fellowship; but much more easier a light-headed young man, as thou art, and such as comes unexperienced out of the country, as now thou doest.

But now being entangled in their fellowship, first pride infects thee with a desire to be as brave[4] as the best; where if thou hast living,[5] either in possession, or possibility, thou shalt find sweet baits amongst them to choke thee withal: for many of these places aforesaid nourish most dangerous and wicked guests, which will quickly close with the inexperienced young man, and

---

3. Eating houses or taverns.
4. Bold, with additional sense of finely dressed.
5. An endowment or property.

of his ability maintain themselves cunningly like gentlemen, which be gallant shifters, cunning panders, and covetous brokers.

First, the gallant shifter, like a cunning companion, in apparel, countenance, and boldness, will checkmate[6] with men of right good worship, when he himself (perhaps) in a green thicket by the highway side, with a masked face, and a pistol, and a whipcord, gets his whole inheritance.

But the manner of such cunning shifts I think necessary to conceal, lest the report prove more hurtful to the evil inclined, than the admonition profitful to the well disposed. But this I assure thee of (as many a gentleman's undoing witnesseth), but these expert shifters, by fast dice, slippery casting, and other like flights dally with young novices so long, till they make their purses a poor penniless banquet.

And (my son) be thou thus conceited,[7] that the man that is enticed to be a dicer, of his own accord will become a whoremaster, where a few of ordinary dinners in that kind will waste a great deal of his substance.

But some will say, the want of acquaintance will keep him chaste: but I conclude with the proverb: "Money will hire a guide to go to the Devil." And surely at such ordinary meetings as be in bowling alleys and dicing houses, a man may find many of these neat panders, such as only live upon brokage of love, fellows that will procure a woman's acquaintance for a dumb man; these be no bashful companions, but such as glory in their base faculty, their common talk will be of ribaldry, and manner of like purpose. And to conclude, he will take advantage of time and place, and cunningly blow a meeting of fair women into my young master's ears, and then his company needeth not to be requested, for presently desire maketh him mad for their meeting. "Where?" he cries, "Come let us go"; and so, with more haste

---

6. Defeat in sense of gull or cheat.
7. Aware

than good speed hies to some blind[8] brothel house about the suburbs, or skirts of the city, where (peradventure) for a pottle or two of wine, the embracement of a painted strumpet, and the French welcome[9] for a reckoning, the young novice payeth 40 shillings or better.

Yet for all this, my brave shifter hath a more costly reckoning to give him, for being thus grown into acquaintance, he will in a familiar kind of courtesy, accompany him up and down the city, and in the end will come unto mercer's or goldsmith's shop, of whom the young gentleman is well known, there will he cheapen[10] velvet, satin, jewels, or what him liketh, and offer his new friend's credit for the payment, he will with so bold a countenance ask this friendship that the gentleman shall be to seek of excuse to deny him. Well, although the pennyworths of the one be not very good, yet the payment of the other is sure to be current.

Thus by prodigal riots, vain company, and rash suretiship,[11] many of our English young gentlemen, as learned to say

I wealthy was of late,
Though needy now be;
Three things have changed my state,
Dice, wine, and venery.

But to our purpose. The delights of these tabling houses are so pleasant and tempting, that a man when he hath there lost all his money, will be most willing, even in the place of his undoing, to stand moneyless, and be an idle looker on, of other men's unthriftiness.

After all this, there seizeth upon the needy gentleman thus

8. Windowless.
9. Venereal disease. The French called V.D. the "English disease."
10. Shop for.
11. Being the one who gives security for loan.

consumed, another devouring caterpillar, which is the broker for money: one that is either an old bankrupt citizen, or some smooth conditioned, unthrifty gentleman far in debt, some one of these will help him to credit with some of their late creditors, with a single protestation of mere courtesy. But by your favor, they will herein deal most cunningly: for the citizen broker (after money taken out for his pains, consideration for the time given, and loss in selling of the wares put together) will bring the young gentleman fifty pounds current money for a hundred pounds good debt.

Many the gentleman broker will deal more gallanter, for he will be bound with his fellow gentleman for a hundred pounds sharing the money equally between them, not without solemn promise to discharge his own fifty, and if need be, the whole hundred pounds assurance.

But let all these mischiefs go: here is want supplied, which breaks brazen walls, and money received, which betrayeth kingdoms, and for the same, nothing but ink, war, and parchment delivered, which is a merry exchange, if a man should be always thus busied in receiving, and never find leisure for the repayment.

But oh thou unhappy young gentleman, whatsoever thou be, that art thus matched, here must I breathe awhile, and admonish thee with a few notes of my counsel of experience: for I know thy covetous desire of money is such, and so great, that thou hadst rather become debtor for forty pounds, than to spare forty shillings out of thy purse: therefore, take this lesson from a tongue of experience. Thou wert better give one of these fellows ten pounds, than to be bound for fifteen, for what so remaineth thou savest, when all that thou venturest, thou losest: and be thou assured, that thou wilt find no time to satisfy thy covenant, yet will thy creditor work thee an arrest, which (until he be fully contented and paid) will give thee little case, and less liberty. But I fear me, all in vain do I give this counsel to a prodigal,

that is tied to a covetousness with silver links, for prodigality and
covetousness chained together, are two extreme passions, and so
violent, that no physic can cure, but beggary and death: beggary
is the end of prodigality, and death the end of covetousness. Yet
in my mind of them both the covetous man is the worser: for
with his riches he doth no man good, no not so much as himself,
when the prodigal by the undoing of himself enricheth many.
Therefore the best that may be said of the prodigal concludeth an
undoing of himself and his posterity.

I have read in the works of a famous philosopher, which
saith, the prodigal man never observeth time, beginning nor
end, until riot hath consumed him and his patrimony. And where
is it consumed, but in ordinaries, dicing houses, bowling alleys,
and such like assemblies, which if they were suppressed, many
a man's land would be kept from selling, many a man's neck
from the halter, and the Commonwealth (perhaps) from further
mischiefs. And from my heart I wish, that upon the gate or door
of every tabling[12] house and bowling alley might be set a whip
and a halter[13] for a sign, then surely all unthrifts and their associates would be ashamed to come to those places, unless shame
had utterly forsook them.

I have but yet begun to anatomize the head of these sanctu-
aries of iniquity; there are heaps and whole bodies of evils follow:
the deceit of dice, the charge of strumpets, the sleight of cozenage, and the cunning of brokage, is all that I have yet laid out
upon our wild-headed young gentlemen, which (like carrions)
only prey upon gold, silver, and such like carriage;[14] these be
but sucking flies; the biting scorpions come after. Even as a bird
that hath but one feather limed, by striving fettereth her whole
body: so the unfortunate young gentleman, which is brought

---

12. Backgammon.
13. Whip and halter (hangman's noose) were forms of punishment gamblers
might expect to encounter.
14. Goods.

behind hand by the hazard of dice, through a vain hope to redeem himself, followeth his mischief, to the opening of the last payment of all his estate; and then (to help him forward) someone spy of the law, or other: namely, a pettifogger (the reverence done into the law, and good lawyers reverence) is ever more sneaking into the company of rich heirs, and still keeps an alphabet of all such gentlemen's names that frequenteth these common gaming houses; his eyes are settled on their dispositions, and his exercise is daily to search the rolls, and the office of the statutes, to learn what recognizances, mortgages, and statutes do charge their lands.

This is the pernicious broker; the other helped the needy gentleman to money, at fifty in the hundred loss, but he helpeth him to sell land at five years' purchase.

I must here digress from the prodigality of the gentleman, unto the covetousness and usury (I cannot well say) of the citizen, although he dwelleth in the city. For the true citizen (whereof London hath plenty) liveth upon his calling, be he a merchant, venturing abroad, or a tradesman living at home: but these shames of good citizens, I mean such as tradeth but only to a gaming house, or at the furthest, travelleth but to a bowling alley, a horse-rifling,[15] the meeting of gentlemen at an ordinary, and such like.

There with ease and safety do these fellows gather wealth and riches as fast as the good citizen with much hazard, and far travels.

These caterpillars come not thither to play the unthrifts, but to prey upon unthrifts, and yet for company, and to avoid suspicion, they will sometimes play the good fellows, and now and then sport a pound or two.

These men need not to greedily seek for purchases, for the necessity of decaying gentlemen, and young citizens, will make

15. Raffle.

them fair offers, and their spies (as I said before) will give them knowledge where there is found dealing.

Now amongst these fellows there is such deceit colored with cleanly[16] shifts, as many gentlemen are for a trifle shifted out of their livings without hope of recovery. For it is well known that the extremity and hard dealing of such men hath impressed a natural malice in the hearts of gentlemen against citizens, insomuch that if a gentleman proposed to scoff a citizen, he will call him a *trim merchant*. Likewise, the citizen scoffing the gentleman, will call every common fellow a *jolly gentleman*.

Truly, truly, in my mind, this mortal envy between the two worthy estates was first begotten by the cruel usage of covetous merchants in former ages, by hard bargains gotten of gentlemen and still nourished as revenges taken of both parties.

Thus one mischief draws on another, and in my opinion, gaming houses are the chief fountains thereof, which wicked places first nourisheth our young men of England in pride, then acquainteth them with sundry shifting companions, whereof one sort cozeneth them at dice and cards, another sort consume them with riotous meetings, another sort by brokage bringeth them in debt and out of credit, and then awaiteth covetousness and usury to seize on their livings, and the officious sergeant[17] upon their liberties. And all this (as I said before) principally proceeds by the frequenting of gambling houses.

But let us now search deeper into these wounds of a Commonwealth, for if we consider all things aright, there is more fouler matter behind, in such things as makes my heart bleed to think of; we have but yet spoken of those gaming houses, which are chiefly for the entertainment of courtiers and gentlemen; the others be of a most private standing, which be called common houses, where the vulgar and inferior sort of people resort, such

---

16. Clever.
17. Police officer.

as have poor wives and children, and families to care for. Surely the inconvenience cannot choose but be great when a poor man leaveth his house, and the company of his wife and family, and dineth abroad amongst gamesters, whose wits be still laboring which way to deceive him.

This order methinks is a bad order, and a breach of credit, to see a tradesman, or one that gets his living by the sweat of his brows, to eat and drink abroad unless one neighbor invite another, but sufferance hath brought this disorder to such a custom that it is now made a daily practice amongst our poorer sort of citizens. Marry, the masters of these gaming houses want[18] no guests, for where carrion is, crows will be plenty, and where money is stirring, theaters will not be idle.

Young citizens, for the most part, depend upon their credit, and therefore are loath that there should be an open knowledge of their unthriftiness. All the better (I say) for the biting cheater, for close in a chamber one of these cogging knaves getteth more money in an hour than many an honest man spendeth in one year.

But above others, this one thing is much to be lamented: by this vain delight, unthrifty citizens consume other men's goods who (perhaps) labored painfully to get them; when gentlemen, although that they undo their posterity, spend but their own goods and lands.

The ears of the magistrates are daily full of the breaking of young merchants, and here I lay before their eyes, the causes thereof. Even these wicked meeting places may be places unto which magistrates come not, and therefore the abuses unknown unto them, but I think it a work of much bounty to reveal them, and in the magistrate a work of more justice to reform them; and although this be true that I write, and the evils more than I will speak of, yet I find my conscience free from their shifts,

18. Lack.

as I presume that no man (as faulty) will or can reprehend me for those kind of courses, and to keep myself more clear from them, I will pass by those streets where houses are planted, and bless me from enticements from them, which indeed are many and more dangerous, in that they please with a vain hope of gain.

There now comes into my mind, a pretty saying of a distemperate dicer, which solemnly did swear that he believed that dice were made of the bones of a witch, and cards of her skin, in which there hath ever since remained a kind of enchantment, that whosoever once taketh delight in either, shall never have power to utterly leave them. "For," quoth he, "a hundred times have I vowed to leave both, yet have I not the grace to forsake either." But now again to the possibility of reformation to overcome this enticing mischief.

If the magistrates surveyed but these vile houses by honest conservators,[10] you should find the painful travels of capital magistrates much eased, many men's lives shall be saved, gentlemen have more land, and citizens greater store of money, which mettle is the greatest strength of a city, for where money is not scarce, traffic is plenty, which supporteth all cities. But to my purpose; these devilish houses are causes that merchants have so much land, and gentlemen so little government.

I have already shown to what extremity the better sort of these houses bring a number of our flourishing young gentlemen; to what misery the second sort (called *ordinaries* for citizens) bring a great number of young merchants.

Now remaineth the discovery of the third sort of these haunts which are placed in the suburbs of the city, in alleys, gardens, and other obscure corners, out of the common walks of the magistrates. The daily guests of these privy houses are masterless men, needy shifters, thieves, cutpurses, unthrifty servants, both servingmen and prentices. Here a man may pick out mates for

19. Judicial officials.

all purposes save such as are good. Here a man may find out fellows that for a pottle of wine will make no more conscience to kill a man than a butcher a beast. Here closely lie Saint Nicholas's clerks,[20] that with a good northern gelding will gain more by a halter than an honest yeoman will with a team of good horses. Here are they that will not let to deceive their father, to rob their brother, and fire their neighbor's house for an advantage. These brave companions will not stick to spend frankly though they have neither lands nor goods by the dead, nor honesty by nature. But how will this hold out? Fire will consume wood without maintenance, and riot make a weak purse without supply.

Gentlemen (for the most part) have lands to make money, and the young citizens way to get credit; but these idle fellows have neither lands nor credit, nor will live by any honest means or occupations: yet have they lands to filch, heads to deceive, and friends to receive, and by these helps, most commonly, shift they badly well.

The other upon current assurance, perhaps, get money for twenty marks, or twenty pounds in the hundred, but these that worst may hold the candle; they upon their own, or upon their master's apparel, brass, pewter, linen, woolen, or such like, will find brokers or fripperers,[21] that for eight pence in the pound for every month's use will boldly for half the value take these pains.

Surely it seems that this famous city is sore charged with these makeshifts, considering that so many streets and lanes are filled with these petty brokers or cherish-thieves.[22] I pray God that in the principal places and streets of the city there be not of this faculty that will make fifty or threescore pound profit in the hundred, which is sweet gain. I have heard some say that a double

---

20. Highway robbers. St. Nicholas is the patron saint of thieves.
21. Dealers in cast-off clothing.
22. *Cherish* is an adjectival form of *chare,* a back lane.

pawn taketh away the fear of the statute,[23] which is a Jewish usury, and high time to be rooted out of any Christian government.

Some of these kind of covetous usurers are so hard-hearted that I doubt[24] they neither fear God, nor reverence man; neither will they pardon father, nor acknowledge mother, but will make merchandise of their own children. They will neither regard brother or kindred, nor yet keep faith with their friends; but bear false witness, offend the widow, and oppress the orphan. Oh how great is this folly of theirs: to lose life, to seek death, and to banish themselves from heaven eternally.

I have heard some of that profession say that usury (I mean brokage)[25] is turned from a sin to an occupation, because being esteemed as a trade, they would be accounted honest men, but rather in my mind they be termed thieves, for the broker agreeth before, with the borrower, to receive more than was borrowed, because before he steal, he tells the party how much he will steal, as though he stole by law; nay, I may say without law, for like a mystery these brokers have devised more sorts of lending upon pawns than there be tricks at cards, but I am afraid to show you them, lest I should teach you to be of that kind; but yet some few examples will I here venture on, as hereafter followeth, the parties I do know now resident in London.

I know a broker that will take no interest for his money, but will have the lease of your house, or your land, in use, receiving rent for the same till you pay your principal again, which will come to a greater gain than threescore in the hundred.[26]

I know another that will take no interest money, but will have pewter, brass, sheets, plates, tablecloths, napkins, and such like

---

23. The double pawn was a trick (it is no longer known exactly what was done) used to avoid the statute against excessive interest.
24. Fear.
25. Trade of the broker, buying and selling for others for a commission.
26. I.e., sixty-percent interest.

things, to use in his house, till his money come home, which will lose more in the wearing than the interest of the money will come to.

I know another that will take a pawn twice worth the money that he lends, and agree with the borrower to redeem it at a day, or lose it, by which means the poor borrower is forced sometimes for want of money to lose his pawn for half the value.

I know another that will not lend, but buy at small prices, and covenant with the borrower to buy the same again, at such a price, at such a day, or lose it. This is a fellow who seeks to cozen the law, but let him take heed lest the Devil his good master cozens not him, and at the last carry him post into hell.

I know another that will lend out his money to men of occupations, as to butchers, bakers, and such like, upon condition to be his partners in their gains but not in their losses, by which means, he that takes all the pains, and ventures all, is forced to give the broker half the profit for his money.

I know another, for his money lending to a carpenter, a bricklayer, or a plasterer, will agree with them for so many day's work, or so many weeks, for the loan of his money, which if all reckonings be cast will come to a dear interest.

I know many about this city that will not be seen to be brokers themselves, but suffer their wives to deal with their money, as to lend a shilling for a penny a week to fishwives, oyster women, orange wenches, and such like. These be they that look about the city like rats and weasels to gnaw poor people alive, and yet go invisible.

This if it be well considered of is a Jewish brokage,[27] for

27. Until late in the sixteenth century Christian Churches labeled taking any interest on loans *usury,* and forbade it. Jews, whose religion did not prohibit taking interest, made up a substantial proportion of moneylenders. Even though many Christian bankers and merchants charged interest in spite of the prohibition, public prejudice labeled it a Jewish vice. The English civil statute outlawing interest was repealed in 1576, but the prejudice against usury remained for some time. As capitalism replaced the old feudal economic system in England, taking interest became more widespread, as this pamphlet indicates.

indeed the Jews first brought usury and brokage into England, which now by long sufferance have much blemished the ancient virtues of this kingdom: let us but remember this one example, how that in the time of King Henry the Third,[28] citizens of London in one night slew five hundred Jews, for that a Jew took of a Christian a penny in the shilling usury, and even after got them banished the city; but truly these brokers aforesaid deserve worse than Jews, for they be like unto strumpets, for they receive all men's money, as well the beggar's as the gentleman's. Nay, they will themselves take money upon brokage, to bring their trade into a better custom, which in my mind is a wicked custom, to live only by sin.

The good magistrates I hope will overlook[29] these evils, lest these evils overrule their posterity, but especially these tabling houses, wherein so many hundred shifters maintain themselves gallantly, to the undoing of a number of good gentlemen, citizens, tradesmen, and such like. For if the shifters in, and within the level of London, were truly mastered I dare boldly say they would amaze a good army. I would their close coverts[30] were discovered, and then no doubt but justice would find their faults, or repentance show their amendment.

To conclude, it is every man's case in this land that hath care of his posterity to be suitors for reformation; the evil hereof even perisheth the marrow and strength of this happy realm. I mean the ability of the gentry is much weakened and many good citizens almost wasted by haunting of these ungracious houses: if this my discovery be considered a wisdom, I presume it will prove beneficial to this glorious monument of the land, London I mean, which the Lord bless and keep in this her wonted prosperity. Amen.

Finis.

---

28. Ruled 1227–72; the massacre took place Easter Week, 1264.
29. Examine.
30. Secret hiding places.

A Treatise against Painting

Painting, the Elizabethan term for using cosmetics, may seem a peccadillo alongside of murder, witchcraft, and highway robbery—or even swindling—but nonetheless it was a serious concern of Renaissance moralists. It also attracted a good deal of literary comment. Hamlet lashes out at Ophelia: "I have heard of your paintings too, well enough; God has given you one face, and you make yourselves another." In Sonnet 127, Shakespeare complains of

> . . . beauty slander'd with a bastard shame:
> For since each hand hath put on nature's power,
> Fairing the foul with art's false borrowed face,
> Sweet beauty hath no name, no holy bower,
> But is profan'd, if not lives in disgrace.

Ben Johnson has a lengthy satire of the burgeoning cosmetic industry in *The Devil Is an Ass.*

The prime objection to painting was that it was a reflection of vanity—the pursuit of absolutely worthless things—when the lady should have been concerned with the welfare of her soul. Furthermore, moralists argued, painting meant defacing God's handiwork. And, of course, they were aware that the end of painting was sexual attraction; the "plastering art," as Claudius calls it in *Hamlet,* was invariably practiced in the brothel. The term *painted lady* has lasted even until our time as a euphemism for a prostitute.

Knowledge of chemistry was limited during the Renaissance, and accordingly cosmetology was a pretty crude art by modern standards. One technique called for painting the face and neck with a white paint, adding rouge when it dried.

176

Painting occasionally proved dangerous to the body as well as the soul. In their desperation to be beautiful, women sometimes risked using poisonous substances like mercury sublimate—often with disastrous results.

Our pamphlet is more eclectic and pedantic than most Elizabethan tracts. Before Tuke gets down to his attack he includes more than twenty epigrams and poems, and a translation of a Spanish tract. His own work is a patchwork of quotes from the Fathers of the Church and other theological authorities, many of them blatantly antifeminist. The pamphlet ends with a short sketch, called a *character,* describing the salient features of a commonly encountered type of individual, in this case a painted lady. The character, which may be traced ultimately to Theophrastus, was quite popular during the Renaissance, the best-known collection of characters being that of Sir Thomas Overbury.

A TREATISE AGAINST PAINTING AND TINCTURING OF MEN AND WOMEN

To Women that Paint Themselves

A loam wall and painted face are one;
For the beauty of them both is quickly gone.
When the loam is fallen off, then lathes appear,
So wrinkles in that face from th'eye to th'ear.
The chastest of your sex contemn these arts,
And many that use them have rid in carts.[1]

Arthur Dowton.

To Painted Women

Stay women—Gallants, cast an eye aside,
See where a mirror represents your pride.
Not that your fardingales[2] fill too much room,
Nor that your lofty tires[3] you misbecome:

---

1. I.e., to prison or execution.
2. Framework of hoops used for extending skirts of women's dresses.
3. Ornamental headdress.

A
TREATISE
AGAINST PAIN-
TNG AND TINCTVRING
OF MEN AND WOMEN:

Against
$\left\{\begin{array}{l}\textit{Murther} \text{ and } \textit{Poysoning :}\\ \textit{Pride} \text{ and } \textit{Ambition :}\\ \textit{Adulterie} \text{ and } \textit{Witchcraft.}\end{array}\right.$

AND THE ROOTE OF ALL THESE,
Disobedience to the Ministery of the word.

WHEREVNTO IS ADDED
The picture of a picture, or, the Character
of a Painted Woman.

By THOMAS TVKE, *Minister of Gods word at*
Saint Giles *in the* Fields.

ROM. 6.
The wages of sinne is death.

Quot vitia, tot venena.
A deceitfull heart hath deceiued them: they consider not
that a lie is in their face.

LONDON,
Printed by *Tho.Creed,* and *Barn.Allsope,* for *Edward*
Merchant dwelling in *Pauls* Church-yard,
neere the Crosse. 1 6 1 6.

Nor paps[4] embossed laid forth to men's view
(Though that be vain too, if wise men say true):
But that ye have renounced your native face,
Under a color that paint adds a grace,
To your enticing looks. But is't no sin,
When vermeil[5] blushes to belie your skin?
Alas what comfort can your looking glass
Yield you, fond creatures, when it comes to pass
That o're the paint is blurred, which makes you fret,
Or ye see nought else but a counterfeit,
A shadow of yourself? Why should you seem
Fairer than women? Men oft misesteem
Your sweetest beauties: for because they know
Some of you are less beauteous than they show.
And who would willingly her beauty saint[6]
Whose face ill-colored is clouded o're with paint?
If ye be fair, what need of new complexion?
If black, or wrinkled, learn what a confection
The first, that was a moralist doth learn you;
Be virtuous, a bad face will nothing yerne[7] you.
Who would be ugly in heaven's piercing sight,
To seem fair to some mortal partial wight?[8]
Yet none so partial, but he needs must see
Upon your brow folly and vanity
In their own colors: and 'tis hard to find
A painted face sort[9] with a single[10] mind.

Ed. Tylnean.

---

4. Breasts.
5. Vermillion.
6. Consider saintly or holy.
7. Earn.
8. Person.
9. Consort.
10. Simple, honest, sincere.

Of tincturing the face

To what may I a painted wench compare?
She's one disguised, when her face is bare.
She is a sickly woman always dying.
Her color's gone, but more she is a-buying.
She is a rainbow, colors altogether,
She makes fair shew, and bears us all fair weather:
And like a bow: she's flexible to bend,
And is led in a string by any friend.
She is Medea, who by likelihood
Can change old Aeson into younger blood,[11]
Which can old age in youthful colors bury,
And make Proserpine[12] of an hag, or fury.
She's a physician well skilled in complexions,
The sick will soon look well by her confections.
She's a false coiner, who on brazen face,
Or copper nose can set a guilded grace.
And though she doth an hood, like ladies, wear,
She bears two faces under't I dare swear.
When hosts of women walk into the field,
She must the ancient[13] be, we all must yield.
For she doth bear the colors all men know,
And flourishes with them, and makes a show.
And to conclude, she'll please men in all places:
For she's a mimic, and can make good faces.

Tho. Drayton

---

11. Medea restored Aeson's youth by letting his blood and replacing it with a potion of her own decoction.

12. Beautiful daughter of Ares, carried off into the underworld by Pluto.

13. Flag, colors.

THE INVECTIVE OF DOCTOR ANDREAS DE LAGUNA, A SPAN-
IARD AND PHYSICIAN TO POPE JULIUS THE THIRD, AGAINST
THE PAINTING OF WOMEN, IN HIS ANNOTATIONS UPON
DIOSCORIDES,[14] BOOK 5, SECTION 62.

The ceruse of white lead, wherewith women use to paint themselves, was without doubt brought in use by the Devil, the capital enemy of nature, therewith to transform human creatures of fair, making them ugly, enormous, and abominable. For certainly it is not to be believed that any simple women without a great inducement and instigation of the Devil, would ever leave their natural and graceful countenances, to seek others that are suppositions and counterfeits, and should go up and down whited and sized[15] over with paintings laid one upon another, in such sort: that a man might easily cut off a curd or cheesecake from either of their cheeks. Amongst which unhappy creatures, there are many who have so betard[16] their faces with these mixtures and flubbersauces, that they have made their faces of a thousand colors: that is to say, some as yellow as the marigold, others a dark green, others blunket color,[17] others as of a deep red dyed in the wool. O desperate madness, O hellish invention, O devilish custom: can there be any greater dotage or sottishness in the world, than for a woman in contempt of nature (who like a kind mother gives to every creature whatsoever is necessary to it in its kind) to cover her natural face, and that pure complexion which she has received, with stench of plasters and cataplasms. What shall God say to such in the Last Judgment, when they shall appear thus masked before him with these antifaces: "Friends, I know you not, neither do I hold you for my creatures: for these are not the faces that I formed." Thus the use of this

---

14. First-century A.D. Greek physician.
15. Size is a gluey substance used to prepare materials to be printed.
16. Smeared with tar.
17. Greyish blue.

ceruse, besides the rotting of the teeth, and the unsavory breath which it causes, being ministered in paintings, doth turn fair creatures into infernal furies. Wherefore let all gentlewomen and honorable matrons, that make prize of their honesty and beauty, leave these base arts to the common strumpets, of whom they are fittest to be used, that by that filthiness they may be known and noted. Yet do I not altogether mislike, that honest women should wash themselves, and seek to make their faces smooth, but that they should use the barley water, or the water of lupines,[18] or the juice of lemons, and infinite other things, which Dioscorides prescribes as cleanly, and delicate to clear the face, and not go continually with rank smells of ointments and plasters about them. Howbeit that you may not think that this unhappy trade and practice of painting is altogether new and of late brought into the world, I will recount unto you a story which Galen[19] alleges in a little book of his, which he entitles, "An exhortation to good arts." Phryne, a famous harlot of Athens, being present at a great feast or banquet, where every one of the guests might by turns command what he pleased to the rest there united, she, seeing many women there that were painted with ceruse, enjoined that they should execute her command very severely, which was, that they should bring a bowl full of warm water, and that they should all wash their faces therein, which was done without gainsaying, for that was the law of the feast. Whereupon the faces of all the women there present appeared foully deformed and stained over, the painting running down their cheeks to their utter shame and confusion, and the horror of all that stood by, to whom they seemed and appeared as horrible monsters, only Phryne appeared much more beautiful and fair than before: for albeit her life were not free from blame, yet was her beauty and comely grace pure, natural, and without artifice, but God be

18. Flowering plant.
19. Second-century Greek physician known for scientific and medical writings.

thanked, said he, our ladies of Spain are so fair of themselves, that they have no need of anything to clear their complexions, but only a little orpine and soliman, or mercury sublimate.

Now that you may know that he flouts his countrywomen, hear what he said of this soliman[20] in his annotation upon the sixty-ninth chapter. The excellency of this mercury sublimate (said he) is such, that the women, who often paint themselves with it, though they be very young, they presently turn old with withered and wrinkled faces like an ape, and before age comes upon them, they tremble (poor wretches) as if they were sick of the staggers, reeling, and full of quicksilver, for so are they: for the soliman and quicksilver differ only in this, that the soliman is the more corrosive and biting; insomuch that being applied to the face, it is true, that it eats out the spots and stains of the face, but so, that with all, it dries up, and consumes the flesh that is underneath, so that of force the poor skin shrinks, as they speak of the famous pantofle[21] of an ancient squire called Petro Capata, which being often besmeared over to make it black, and to give it luster, it shrunk and wrinkled, and became too short for his foot. This harm and inconvenience (although it be great), yet it might well be dissembled, if others greater than this did not accompany it; such as are, a stinking breath, the blackness and corruption of the teeth which this soliman engenders. For if quicksilver alone, applied only to the soles of the feet, once or twice, and that in a final quantity, doth mar and destroy the teeth, what can be expected from the soliman, which is without comparison more powerful and persistive, and is applied more often, and in greater quantity to the very lips and cheeks? So that the infamous inconveniences which result from this mercury sublimate, might be somewhat the more tolerable, if they did stick and stay only in them who use it, and did not descend

20. Mercuric chloride. This passage indicates that mercury poisoning was a problem long before the twentieth century.
21. Slipper.

to their offspring. For this infamy is like to original sin, and goes from generation to generation, when as the child born of them, before it be able to go, doth shed his teeth one after another, as being corrupted and rotten, not through his fault, but by reason of the viciousness and taint of the mother that painted herself, who, if she loath and abhor to hear this, let her forbear to do the other.

Translated out of Spanish by Mist. Elizabeth Arnold.

OF PAINTING THE FACE

Though these times and places, in which we now live, are stained with fouler faults than this of which I have taken upon me here to entreat, yet because it was (as I suppose) never so common, as it is now amongst us, and seeing by connivance, or silence, it still delates[22] itself, and now at length finds some friends, which stick not in corners either to defend it, or to extenuate the vileness of it, I have therefore singled it out alone from many other vanities, against which many have bent themselves by word and writing, purposing to declare unto the world what I am able to say against it, entreating all with judgment to ponder what I write, and if they shall perceive my reasons sound and good, to join together with me in the persecution and banishing of this evil from amongst us, of whom better things are looked for, and desired. And I humbly beseech Almighty God to direct my heart and hand, that I may think and write that which shall be pleasing to Him, and to prosper and bless it unto all that shall read or hear it, that it may find friendly entertainment in their hearts, and produce fruits answerable to it in their lives and practice.

22. Accuses, indicts.

A
DISCOVRSE
Againſt Painting and
Tincturing of WOMEN.

Wherein the abo-minable ſinnes of	{ Murther *and* Poyſoning, Pride *and* Ambition, Adultery *and* Witchcraft, }	are ſet foorth & diſcouered.

Robert *Gordon*

Whereunto is added the Picture of a Picture, or,
The Character of a Painted Woman.

¶ Imprinted at *London* for *Edward Marchant*. 1616.

Saint Paul, inspired with the Spirit of Christ, gives a golden precept, to which if we will yield obedience, as we should, we shall willingly abstain from this artificial facing. "Whatsoever things" (saith he) "are true, whatsoever things are venerable, whatsoever things are just, whatsoever things are (chaste or) pure, whatsoever things are lovely, whatsoever things are of good report: if there be any virtue, and if there be any praise, think on these things." These things he would have us to delight in, and to do: the contrary he would have us decline, and abandon. But a painted face is a false face, a true falsehood, not a true face. "That picture," said St. Ambrose,[23] "that picture [or painting] is of corruption, and not comely, that painting is deceitful, and not of simplicity, that painting lasts but a while, it is wiped off either with rain or sweat: that painting deceives and beguiles, that it can neither please him, whom thou desires to please, who perceiveth this pleasing beauty to be none of thine, but borrowed: and thou dost also displease thy maker, who seeth his work to be defaced."

Or is this painting venerable, or venerous[24] and abominable rather? Do men of worth and judgment respect and favor it, as a thing honest, and worthy to be esteemed? Did ever patriarch, prophet, apostle, or Father of the Church approve it? Hath it not been ever scorned of sage and grave men? A painted face is not much unlike an idol; it is not that it would be taken for: and they, that make it, are like unto it, and so are all they that do delight therein, and worship it.

Shall we say the painting of hair or face is just? Doth the law of God require or favor it? Or doth reason uncorrupted teach it? Or have the laws of any wise and understanding heads endured or enjoined it? Or rather is it not altogether injurious? Sure there is a wrong, done to God, whose workmanship they would

---

23. Fourth-century Church Father, Bishop of Milan.
24. Lustful.

seem to mend, being discontented with it. St. Hierome[25] saith, "She paints herself by a glass, and to the contumely of her Creator labors to be fairer than she was born." And in an epistle to Laeta concerning the institution of her daughter, where he related a story of a certain woman grievously smitten for painting of her daughter, he called those that do such things, violaters of the Temple of Christ. Saint Origen[26] likewise taxes painted women by sundry places of Scripture, among other things, for daubing their living face with dead colors, and affirms, that they do these things *in contumeliam Creatoris,* to the disgrace of their Creator. Saint Ambrose also thus writes to the same effect: "Thou art painted, O man, and painted of the Lord thy God. Thou hast a good Artisan and Painter: do not deface that good picture (*non fuco, sed veritate fulgentem*) shining not with deceitful stuff, but with true colors. O woman, thou defacest the picture, if thou daubest thy countenance with material whiteness, or a borrowed red. Tell me, if after one workman has done, thou usest the help of another to overlay the work of the former with his new devices, doth he not take it in ill part, who sees his work to be disguised? Do not take away God's picturing, and assume the picture of a harlot, because it is written, 'Shall I take the members of Christ, and make them the members of an harlot?' God forbid. If any man adulterate the work of God, he committeth a grievous offense. For it is an heinous crime to think that man can paint thee better than God. It is a grievous thing that God should say of thee, I see not the image, I see not the countenance, which myself have formed, I reject that, which is not mine. Seek him that hath painted thee, deal with him, take grace of him to whom thou hast given a reward. What answer wilt thou make him? . . ."

---

25. St. Jerome, fifth-century Church Father.
26. 185–254, Christian philosopher and scholar.

THE PICTURE OF A PICTURE
OR
THE CHARACTER OF A PAINTED WOMAN

She is a creature that has need to be twice defined; for she is not that she seems. And though she be the creature of God, as she is a woman, yet is she her own creatress, as a picture. Indeed a plain woman is but half a painted woman, who is both a substantive and an adjective, and yet not of the neuter gender: but a feminine as well consorting with a masculine, as ivy with an ash. She loves grace so well, that she will rather die than lack it. There is no truth with her to favor, no blessing to beauty, no conscience to contentment. A good face is her god: and her cheek well dyed is the idol she doth so much adore. Too much love of beauty hath wrought her to love painting: and her love of painting hath transformed her into a picture. Now her thoughts, affections, talk, study, work, labor, and her very dreams are on it. Yet all this makes her but a cinnamon tree, whose bark is better than her body; or a piece of gilded copper offered for current gold. She loves a true looking glass, but to commend age, warts, and wrinkles, because otherwise she cannot see to lay her falsehood right. Her body is (I ween)[27] of God's making: and yet it is a question; for many parts thereof she made herself. View her well, and you'll say her beauty's such, as if she had bought it with her penny. And to please her in every of her toys, would make her maid run besides her wits, if she had any. She's ever amending, as a beggar's apiecing, yet is she for all that no good penitent. For she loves not weeping. Tears and mourning would mar her making: and she spends more time in powdering, pranking,[28] and painting, than in praying. She's more in her ointments

27. Believe.
28. Dressing up.

a great deal, than in her orizons.[29] Her religion is not to live well, but die[30] well. Her piety is not to pray well, but to paint well. She loves confections better a great deal than confessions, and delights in facing and feasting more than fasting. Religion is not in so great request with her as riches: not wealth so much as worship. She never chides so hostilely, as when her box is too secke,[31] her powder's spilt, or her clothes ill set on. A good bed-friend she is commonly, delighting in sheets more than in shoes, making long nights, and short days. All her infections are but to gain affections, for she had rather die than live and not please. Her lips she lays with so fresh a red, as if she sang, "John come kiss me now." Yet it's not out of love, excepting selflove, that she so seeks to please, but for love, nor from honesty, but for honor, it is not piety, but praise that spurs her. She studies to please others, but because she would not be displeased herself. And so she may fulfill her own fancy, she cares not who else she doth befool. A name she prefers to nature, and makes more account of fame than faith. And though she do affect singularity, yet she loves plurality of faces. She is nothing like herself, save in this, that she is not like herself. She seldom goes without a pair of faces, and she's furnished with stuff to make more if need be. She says a good archer must have two strings to his bow, but she has hers bent both at once: Yet you must not say, she wears two faces under one hood; for that she's left long since to t'hawks,[32] and has got her headgear that pleases her better; not because better, but newer. Her own sweet face is the book she most looks upon; this she reads over duly every morning, especially if she be to show herself abroad that day: and as her eye

29. Prayers.
30. With a pun on *dye*.
31. Dry (?)
32. The hawks. Hoods were often put over hawks' eyes when the birds were being carried.

or chambermaid teaches her, sometimes she blots out pale, and writes red. The face she makes in the day, she usually mars in the night, and so it's to make a new the next day. Her hair's seldom her own, or if the substance, then not the show, and her face likes her not, if not borrowed. And as for her head, that's dressed, and hung about with toys and devices, like the sign of a tavern, to draw on such as see her. And sometimes is written on her forehead, as on the Dolphin at Cambridge, in capital letters, *èpithi, è apithi*,[33] like or look off. She's marriageable and fifteen at a clap,[34] and afterward she doth not live but long. And if she survive her husband, his going is the coming of her tears, and the going of her tears is the coming of another husband. 'Tis but in dock, out nettle.[35] By that time her face is mended, her sorrows ended. There's no physic[36] she so loves, as face physic: and but assure her she'st ne're need other, while she lives, and she'll die for joy. Rather then she leave her yellowbands,[37] and give over her pride, she will not stick to deny that Mistress Turner[38] spoke against them, when she died. Her devotion is a fine apparel dear bought, and a fine face lately borrowed, and newly set on. These carry her to church, and clear her of recusancy.[39] Once in she unpins her mask, and calls for her book, and now she's set. And if she have any more devotion, she lifts up a certain number of eyes towards the preacher, rises up, stands a while, and looks about her: then turning her eyes from beholding vanities (such as she herself brings with her) she sits down, falls a-nodding, measures out a nap by the hourglass, and awakes

---

33. Greek: "either drink up or get out"—an old Persian saying.
34. Marriageable as soon as she is fifteen.
35. Dock is an herb supposed to help in removing nettles. The expression means that one thing replaces another painlessly.
36. Medicine.
37. Word unknown.
38. Anne Turner (1576–1615) was involved in the murder of Sir Thomas Overbury. She was hanged at Tyburn.
39. Refusing to attend church.

to say, "Amen." She delights to see, and to be seen: for her labor's more than half lost, if nobody should look upon her. She takes a journey now and then to visit a friend, or see a cousin: but she never travels more merrily than when she is going to London. London, London hath her heart. The Exchange[40] is the temple of her idols. In London she buys her head, her face, her fashion. O London, thou art her Paradise, her Heaven, her all in all! If she be unmarried, she desires to be mistaken, that she may be taken. If married to an old man, she is rather a reed and a rack unto him, than a staff and a chair, a trouble rather than a friend, a corrosive, not a comfort, a consumption, not a counselor. The utmost reach of her providence is but to be counted lovely, and her greatest envy is at a fairer face in her next neighbor; this, if anything, makes her have sore eyes. She is little within herself, and hath small content of her own; and therefore is still seeking rather than enjoying. All is her own, you see, and yet in truth nothing is her own almost, you see; not her head, her hair, her face, her breasts, her scent, nay, not her breath always. She hath purchased lips, hair, hands, and beauty more than nature gave her, and with these she hopes to purchase love. For in being beloved consists her life; she is a fish that would fain be taken; a bird that had rather a great deal be in the hand than a bush. These purchases she uses to make, are not of lands, but looks; not of lives, but loves. Yet usually the love she meets with is as changeable as her face, and will not tarry on her, though she die for't. She spends more in face-physic and trifles than in feeding the poor. And so she may be admired herself, she cares not though all her neighbors round about her were counted kitchenstuff. A good huswife[41] takes not more pleasure in dressing her garden with variety of herbs and flowers, than in

40. The Royal Exchange, central meeting place for British merchants.
41. *Housewife* had a perjorative meaning in the sixteenth century. It was closer to *hussy*, which is derived from it, than it is to the present sense of the term.

tricking herself with toys and gauds. Here she is costly, if anywhere. 'Tis her grace to be gay and gallant. And indeed like an
ostrich, or bird of paradise, her feathers are more worth than
her body. The worst piece about her is in the middest. For the
tailor, and her chambermaid, and her own skill, even these
three, are the chiefest causes of all her perfections. Not truths,
but shadows of truths she is furnished with; with seeming truths,
and with substantial lies. Yet with all her fair shows she is but
like a piece of coarse cloth with a fine glass, or fairo die;[42] or as
the herb molio, which carries a flower as white as snow, but is
carried upon a root as black as ink. Her first care in the morning
is to make her a good face, and her last care in the evening is
to have her box, and all her implements ready against the next
morning. She is so curious, and full of business, that two such
in a house would keep the nimblest-fingered girl in the parish
she lives in from making herself one cross-cloth[43] in a twelve-
month. She is so deep in love with toys, that without them she
is but half herself: and half oneself, you know, is not one's self.
She loses herself in her self, that she may find herself in a picture.
Her trade is tincturing, and her luster is her life. You kill her,
if you will not let her die. The hyacinth, or heliotropium, follows
not the sun more duly than she vanity. Pride, which is accidental
to a woman, and hateful to a virtuous woman, is essential to her.
Her godliness is not to do well, but to go well. Her care is not
to live well, but to look well. And yet if she live well, she'll
give you leave to chide her, if she look ill. She so affects the titles
of illustrious and gracious, that she carries them always in print
about her. Her imagination is ever stirring, and keeps her mind
in continual motion, as fire doth the pot a playing, or as the
weights do the jack[44] in her kitchen. Her devices follow her

42. Faro is a game played with cards, not dice. Perhaps this is a variation.
The phrase refers to something fair without and ugly within.
43. Linen forehead band.
44. Small mechanical appliance.

fancy, as the motion of the seas do the moon. And nothing pleases her long, but that which pleases her fancies, with one of which she drives out another, as boys do pellets in elderne guns.[45] She thinks 'tis false to say, that any woman living can be damned for these devices: and it may be true she thinks. For so long as she lives, she cannot: but if she die in them there's the question. She is ever busy, yet never less busy than when she's best busy. She's always idle, yet never less idle than when she is most idle. Once a year at least she would fain see London, though when she comes there, she hath nothing to do, but to learn a new fashion, and to buy her a periwig, powder, ointments, a feather, or to see a play. One of her best virtues is that she respects none that paint: and the reward of her painting is to be respected of none that paint not. If she be a maiden, she would fain be rid of that charge? If a widow, she's but a conterfeit relique; 'twere too gross superstition but to kiss or touch her.[46] Old age still steals upon her unawares: which she discerns not by increase of wisdom, but of weakness, nor by her long-living, but by her need of dying. To conclude, whosoever she be, she is but a gilded[47] pill, composed of these two ingredients, defects of nature, and an artificial seeming of supply, tempered and made up by pride and vanity, and may well be reckoned among these creatures, that God never made. Her picture is now drawn out, and done.

Finis

---

45. Probably slingshots.
46. Kissing relics of Christ or the saints was a Catholic custom looked down upon in England after the Reformation.
47. I.e., candy coated.

A Short Treatise
against Stage Plays

Shakespeare has so long been deified in our country—taught with reverence in the high schools, and even quoted from the pulpit—that it seems strange to us that in his own lifetime many of his fellow citizens wanted to shut down the theaters for moral reasons, thereby depriving the world of *Hamlet, King Lear,* and *Romeo and Juliet,* as well as the plays of his great contemporaries. Ironically the citizens who were determined to do this (and eventually did) were the Puritans, the founders of America.

The Puritans objected to drama for several reasons. For one thing, there were no actresses; female parts were taken by young boys dressed up as women. The Bible expressly forbids transvestitism (Deut. 22:5), and though one feels certain that the Hebrew lawgivers had something else in mind than the harmless exercises of the Elizabethans, the literal-minded Puritans were sticklers for following Scripture to the letter.

Another objection stemmed from the nature of the plays. Elizabethan humor was often coarse, and comedies abounded in sexual and scatalogical jokes. Cuckold jokes were a particular favorite of the period, and there were few comedies that did not have numerous references, puns, and jokes about the invisible horns that supposedly grew on the head of the victimized husband. Tragedies, of course, dealt with murder, treason, and the like, and Puritans thought that this was dangerous stuff for the public to see. Furthermore, Puritans, and everyone else, were aware that a lot of monkey business went on at plays: pickpockets practiced their trade, adulterers made assignations, and drinkers drank.

Finally, there was the economic objection: Puritans mainly came from the newly emerging urban middle class. They were chiefly shopkeepers and artisans. Most theaters put on plays during the afternoon, and businessmen objected strongly to having so many of their potential customers tied up at a theater when they might be out shopping. They also objected to having a freely available distraction for their young apprentices, who were fond of attending performances.

The actors and dramatists, for their part, had little sympathy for the Puritans, and often pilloried them on the stage. Shakespeare's Malvolio is perhaps the best-known lampoon of a Puritan. Ben Johnson's Zeal of the Land Busy is also a marvelous satirical portrait. In *Bartholomew Fair* Busy debates the legitimacy of the theater with a puppet, who thoroughly confounds and humilates him.

Ironically, Puritan opposition to the theater contributed in no small part in making the theater decadent. The Puritans steadily gained converts in the middle class, and these proselytes abandoned the theater. The nature of the audience changed from a broadly based cross section of the nation to a small coterie of sophisticates. These seventeenth-century jet setters found the work of bourgeois playwrights like Shakespeare too wholesome for their jaded palates, and responded instead to the dacadent wares of Marston, Chapman, and Tourneur.

When the Puritans became strong enough to wage, and win, a Civil War against the Royalists, the theater was doomed. In 1642 the Puritan Parliament, in order to "avert the wrath of God," ordered that "public stage-plays shall cease and be forborne." The theaters remained closed until the Restoration of the monarchy in 1660.

A SHORT TREATISE AGAINST STAGE PLAYS:

It is a sport to a fool to do mischief. (Prov. 10:23.)
He that loves pastime shall be a poor man. (Prov. 21:17.)
Have no fellowship with the unfruitful works of darkness, but rather reprove them. (Eph. 5:11.)
Printed in the year of our Lord 1625.

An Humble Supplication Tendred to the High and Honorable House of Parliament Assembled May xviij. 1625.

SHORTE TREATISE
against
STAGE·PLAYES

Prov. 10. 23.
It is a sport to a foole to doe mischief.

Prov. 21. 17.
He that loues pastime shall be a poore man.

Ephef. 5. 11.
Haue no fellowship with the vnfruitfull works of darknesse, but rather reproue them.

Printed in the yeere of our Lord 1625.
✳ ✳ ✳

    Whereas stage plays are repugnant to the written work and will of Almighty God, the only wise governor and righteous judge of the whole world; dangerous to the eternal salvation both of the actors and spectators; breed many inconveniences wheresoever they come; procure the judgments of God to the whole kingdom, for sin tolerated purchaseth God's wrath to the whole nation, as appeareth Joshua 22:18, and Solomon saith Proverbs 14:34. Sin is a reproach to any people; and have been justly censured and worthily prohibited by statutes made in the late reign of famous Queen Elizabeth, and of our learned and noble King James: May it therefore please this High and Honorable House, which is the most honorable court in all Europe, upon view of this short treatise following, to take once more into consideration this matter of stage plays, and by some few words added to the former statutes, to restrain them forever hereafter.

The Preface

In all ages the prophets have applied their preachings to the present occasions: and the general concourse of many baptized Christians to stage plays, everywhere in these times, have occasioned the Lord's remembrancers, which stand continually on their watchtowers, both more diligently to examine the nature of stage plays, which have had much countenance, and some defense; to try whether they be warrantable by the word of God or no; and also more earnest prayer to God for his assistance, and serious endeavors to dissuade Christians from entertaining them. Hence proceed these few ensuing reasons, briefly contracted into a narrow room, that the reader may with facility conceive the force of the arguments, and soundly judge of the truth of them. And for better direction to the reader, the whole sum is drawn to these four heads.

First, the original beginning of stage plays is shown: section 2.

Secondly, the end is pointed out for which they were first devised: section 3.

Thirdly, the general matter or argument acted in them, is opened in few words: section 4.

Fourthly, the reasons to prove them unlawful are rendered: section 5.

The Original Beginning of Stage Plays

The first beginning of plays proceeded from those men which were not in the Church of God, when God had appointed man to get his living, with his labor (Gen. 3:19). Juball, the seventh of Cain his race, invented playing on instruments (Gen. 4:21), which (as after) is a lawful recreation. But the invention of diverse sorts of unlawful plays is briefly noted by Plinius,[1] by Eusebius,[2] by Arnobius,[3] by Polydorus Virgilius,[4] by Alexander ab Alexandro,[5] by Caelius Rhodiginus.[6] Whether they grew up first at Lydia in Asia as saith Herodotus[7] or at Athens in Graecia, as Polydorus Virgilius and Volaterranus[8] report, it is not material. Pausanias[9] in *Eliacis* writes that Iphitus[10] was admonished by the oracle of Apollo to restore the Olympic games. Josephus Scaliger's[11] *Poetices* may satisfy all men that desire to read more of this point. About the beginning of the Persian monarchy, which was almost five hundred years afore Christ, and about the time of the Jews' return out of the captivity of Babylon, this miscreant author, always of some hurt, never of any good to Christian or heathen, first came abroad with great solemnity, as it may be gathered by Herodotus. Afterward from those Lydians in Asia, or from the Grecians at Athens, came plays to Rome in the reign of Tarquinius Priscus, as Eusebius notes in his *Chronology* at the year of the world 4602.[12] Her-

---

1. Gaius Plinius Secundus (Pliny the Elder), Roman naturalist, c. A.D. 23–79.
2. Ecclesiastical historian, Bishop of Caesarea, c. 260–c. 340.
3. Early Christian writer, fl. A.D. 300.
4. English historian of Italian extraction, c. 1470–1555.
5. Italian jurist, 1461–1523.
6. Italian classicist, c. 1450–1525.
7. Greek historian, c. 484–425 B.C.
8. Italian encyclopedist, 1452–1522.
9. Second-century A.D. Greek geographer.
10. In Greek mythology, son of Eurytus, killed by Heracles.
11. French philologist, 1540–1609.
12. 616 B.C. The historians obviously differed widely in their chronologies.

manus Contractus[13] at the year of the world 3341[14] notes the same. And Titus Livius,[15] Pomponius Laetus[16] in *Philippo*, Funccius[17] in his worthy *Chronology* at the year of the world 3512,[18] and Herodianus[19] witness how the Romans augmented their plays afterwards.

The first authorized entrance that any such kind of plays or heathen exercise had into the Church of God, seems to be about 170 years before the birth of Christ, when that wicked Jesus affecting heathenism, changed his name into Jason,[20] and for 150 talents of silver purchased a commission of Antiochus Ephphanes, king of Syria, that he might erect a place for heathen exercises at Jerusalem, and train up the youth of the Jews in the customs of the Gentiles. Which exercise though it was not to play on the stage, but for activity of their bodies, yet it may here be observed as an entrance to other heathen customs, and as that which makes way to bring in stage plays afterwards. Then Herod the Great increased heathenish plays and exercises greatly in his days, building one theater at Jerusalem, and another at Caesarea Stratonis.[21] The horrible sins of the Jews cut them off shortly after from being the Church of God, and therefore no more can be said of their heathenish exercises.

How or when plays came into the Christian Church, and who first gave them entertainment, is more incident to this present purpose, and fitter testimony to give evidence hereafter either for them or against them. When the Roman emperors delighted

---

13. German historian, 1013–54.
14. 616 B.C. See n. 12 above.
15. Livy, Roman historian, 59 B.C.–A.D. 17.
16. Italian humanist, 1425–98.
17. Name unknown.
18. 616 B.C. See n. 12 above.
19. Greek historian, fl. third century A.D.
20. Jason, high priest of the Jews, introduced Greek customs and beliefs into Jerusalem in 175 B.C.
21. City in Asia Minor.

too much in all kind of plays, and when Christian religion grew mightily under them in Europe especially, Christians embracing the Gospel could not be altogether ignorant of these stage plays, but sometimes some Christians resorted to these plays, as by the complaints and invectives of some ancient fathers against them, it doth appear. And though secretly by such means plays through Satan's subtlties approached near to the Church door, yet all this while neither the emperor's power thrust them upon the Church, nor the reverend fathers and faithful pastors of those times gave way to such open wickedness by their silence. But when that great scarlet-colored whore of Babylon with her golden cup of abominations in her hand[22] which hath a name written in her forehead, a mystery, great Babylon the mother of whoredoms, and which reigneth over the kings of the earth, was set in Peter's chair at Rome as the Papists say, then did the king of the Locusts, called Abaddon and Apollyon, having the key of the bottomless pit, with full power for such a purpose, set the Church door wide open for sundry sports and plays to enter freely into the house of God, as Platina[23] reported Paulus II[24] did. And that not only in their great solemnities and festivals, which were spent commonly in belly cheer and plays, as Peuccrus[25] writeth of Urbanus IV,[26] much after the fashion of the Israelites, sitting down to eat and drink, and rising up to play: but specially in their rich jubilees,[27] first begun in the Christian Church by Bonifacius VIII in the year of Christ 1300 and afterward continued and hastened by his successors. Of which sports and plays Aven-

22. See Revelation 17.
23. Italian historian, 1421–81.
24. Pope, 1464–71. He provided games, food, and carnivals for the Roman people.
25. Probably Gaspard Peucer, German scholar, 1525–1602.
26. Pope, 1261–64. Established the festival of Corpus Christi, which was celebrated with great pageantry including, in the fourteenth century, the mystery cycles, dramatic performances of biblical subjects.
27. In the Roman Catholic Church, a holy year once in twenty-five years when special privileges were given for a pilgrimage to Rome.

tinus,[28] speaking of Clement VI[29] and Bale[30] in the life of Julius III[31] do write. And thus much shall suffice for the beginning of plays among the Lydians of Asia; and among the Grecians and Romans in Europe; as also for their entrance into the Christian Church, first secretly by the malice of Satan stealing some Christian's affections to such vanities; then openly by the power of that Abaddon of Rome, who besotted men's senses with such fooleries, that he might rob their purses in his rich jubilees.

The End for Which Plays Were Devised

The final cause or end for which the heathen first devised plays was to pacify their angry gods, and so remove some present calamity which vexed them. The Lydians sought by plays to remedy a great famine that was among them, as Herodotus witnesses in *Clio*. The Athenians renewed their plays about the latter end of the Persian monarchy, in the days of Euthydemus,[32] their governor, thereby thinking to remove a grievous pestilence, as saith Diodorus Siculus,[33] also Livius and Paulus Orosius[34] write that the heathen Romans sore afflicted about the same time, with pestilence, by the advice of their idol priests, set forth their stage plays to turn away that affliction, thinking their plays would please their gods.

But Dionysius Halicarnasseus,[35] Arnobius, Pausanias in *Corinthiacis*, Augustinus, Polydorus Virgil and Volaterranus write so plainly and fully of this matter, that the reading of any one of them may satisfy the sober minded, and give them to under-

---

28. Bavarian historian, 1477–1534.
29. Pope, 1342–52.
30. John Bale, virulently anti-Catholic English author, 1495–1563.
31. Pope, 1550–55.
32. Late third century B.C.
33. First-century B.C. Sicilian historian.
34. Iberian priest, theologian, historian, c. 385–420.
35. Greek historian, fl. late first century B.C.

stand, that as Christians by direction out of God's word use prayer and fasting to turn away the Lord's provoked anger: so heathens instructed by the Devil their master thought to remove their afflictions by plays. But the popes of Rome solemnized their festivals and jubilees with all sorts of plays and sports for recreation, and to delight the people with such fooleries.

The Argument of Stage Plays

Whereas stage plays ordinarily go under the name either of tragedies or else of comedies, we are to understand that the argument or matter acted in tragedies is murder, treason, rebellion, and such like, and in comedies is bauderie,[36] cozenage,[37] and mere knavery.

But here some men either merely ignorant (as the most religious and learned are ignorant of many things, for we know but in part (1 Cor. 13:9) or else perversely irreligious, will say, that sometimes the sacred Scripture is or may be acted by players on the stage, and thereby a man may learn more than at a sermon.

But for better information of the ignorant, and more forcible confutation of the perverse and profane, a threefold answer may be given.

First, concerning those persons that so greatly desire to learn religion at stage plays, let them examine their own consciences by their works which are manifest before God and men, and consider themselves in these five points. (1) They seldom come to the Church to learn religion according to God's ordinance, though God command them so to do (Deut. 12:5): "But ye shall seek the place which the Lord your God shall choose out of all your tribes, to put his name there, and there to dwell, and

36. Bawdry, obscenity.
37. Fraud.

thither thou shalt come"; though God entreat them so to do
(Prov. 1:20): "Wisdom crieth without: she uttereth her voice
in the streets"; as also Proverbs 9:3, and though they promised
at their baptism so to do. (2) They read the Scriptures little or
never at home, they catechise not their families (Deut. 6, 7) or
they are not catechised themselves. (3) They have little or no
delight to confer and talk of religion, but rather are weary of
such as speak to them of religion, avoid their company, and call
them Puritans. (4) They lead not their life religiously, but
follow the fashion of the world either one way or other. (5) They
resort not to stage plays to learn religion, but to solace themselves in sin.

Secondly, concerning the stage players: (1) They are no great
divines, no doctors of divinity, scarce good professors of religion.
(2) They are not called of God to any such public function, as
to be teachers of religion. (3) They are forbidden to meddle
with religion: "What hast thou to do to declare mine ordinances
that thou shouldst take my name in thy mouth, seeing thou
hatest to be reformed, and hast cast my words behind thee?"
(Ps. 50:16). (4) They abuse Scripture when they rehearse it
upon the stage, as conjurers and witches do in their enchant-
ments, charms, sorceries, and conjurations. (5) They pollute
Scripture when they mention it upon the stage. For as the priest
answered that if a polluted person touched the sacrifice, the
oblation should be unclean: so if these stage players meddle with
Scripture they pollute it (Hag. 2:14).

Thirdly, concerning the Scripture itself: (1) God ordained
not that the Holy Scriptures should be acted upon the stage, in
such kind of scurrility, by such light and vain persons, not to
such end as to make sport and pastime; but with great reverence
to be soberly handled, by faithful and lawful ministers, in the
holy assemblies of the saints. (2) The Scripture is God's power
to beat down sin, and not to maintain it; to beget faith, not to

destroy it; to bring men into God's glorious kingdom, and not to throw them down into hell. (3) God smote one Theopompus, an infidel, with lunacy, for inserting Scripture in his writings, and one Theodoctes with blindness for citing Scripture in his tragedy, as it is reported by Josephus[38] and by Eusebius.[39]

Wherefore it is a profane thing to deal with Scripture upon the stage, or in any sport and play, it is pernicious to the actors, hearers, and beholders.

The Reasons Which Prove Stage Plays to Be Unlawful

The first reason shall be taken from their original beginning, which was from the heathen, and to pacify their idol's anger, that present afflictions might be removed, as hath been shown before (section 3). And therefore they seem unlawful for Christians, whom the Apostle warns to avoid, not only that which is evil, but also the very show of evil: "Abstain from all appearance of evil" (1 Thess. 5:22). And in another place he says: "Furthermore, brethren, whatsoever things are true, whatsoever things are honest, whatsoever things are just, whatsoever things are pure, whatsoever things pertain to love, whatsoever things are of good report, if there be any virtue, or if there be any praise, think on these things" (Phil. 4:8). Wherefore seeing there are none of these things in stage plays, and that they bring with them not only appearance of evil, but evil itself, they may not be counted lawful for Christians.

But some will say, we have no respect to their heathenish beginning or use, but now they serve only for recreation, and not otherwise.

The answer first shows what are lawful recreations, and secondly confuteth the objection.

---

38. Jewish historian, 37–95 A.D.
39. Greek Church historian, c. 263–339.

Recreation is a mere compound Latin word, made English by use, and signifies to renew, to repair, to recover, to restore, or to refresh either the body, or the mind, or both, when they are impaired, overworn, wearied, in the employments of men's lawful callings, to the end that men recreated (for it seems convenient to retrain the word) and refreshed, may cheerfully return to their lawful callings again, and therein serve God faithfully. Wherefore here are three things to be considered.

First, that recreations are not always necessary, nor to be permitted to all persons, but only to those that are overwearied with honest labor in their lawful callings.

Secondly, that recreations serve only to refresh men, and make them fitter for the duties of their callings.

Thirdly, some recreations, which the Lord our gracious God, and merciful Father hath in his wisdom and love to his servants granted and thought meet for the sons of men, are particularly to be mentioned, and namely these five especially:

First, some little rest from labor, as if the reapers in harvest time may sit down and rest themselves for one quarter of an hour, they will return more freshly to their work again. And so it is with all other men, in what calling soever they are occupied.

Secondly, food, meat, and drink, which refresh man comfortably, and make him fitter and more able to perform the duties of his calling.

Thirdly, sleep renews man and refreshes him greatly, that he is thereby, as if he had not been wearied before.

Fourthly, some change of labor quickens a man, that his former weariness is forgotten.

Fifthly, music is a cheerful recreation to the mind, that hath been blunted with serious meditations.

These and such like are holy and good recreations both comfortable and profitable, whereunto may be added holy conference of good men concerning good and necessary matters.

As for hawking, hunting, fishing, fowling, and such like, they are rather to be counted honest and lawful callings, wherein men may get their living with their labor, than recreations, except it be by change of labor, as in other lawful callings.

And now to come to confutation of the objection, it seems that stage plays cannot be counted in the number of recreations, and that for these three reasons.

First, they are not worthy to be compared to any of the former lawful recreations.

Secondly, they serve not the end of recreations, which is to refresh the weary, but not to make men delight in sin.

Thirdly, the most persons that ordinarily resort to them, are very idle persons, that should rather be set to some honest labor, than so unprofitably to mispend their time to their own hurt.

The original beginning then is sufficient to persuade the faithful to renounce stageplays, and say unto them, "Get thee hence" (Isa. 30:22).

The second reason may be taken from the matter or argument which is acted upon the stage, which is either murder and mischief in tragedies, or bauderie and cozenage in comedies, as was observed before (section 4). And the reason may be contrived thus.

It is not lawful for Christians to sport themselves either with the dreadful judgments of God, or with the abominable sins of men.

But in stage plays there are acted sometimes the fearful judgments of God, as in tragedies: and sometimes the vile and hateful sins of men, as in comedies.

And therefore it is full of horror seriously to think upon them, and much more to be either actor to show them, or beholder and hearer to laugh at them, or delight in them.

Ham derided his father's nakedness but he was accursed for

it (Gen. 9:22). Curses are denounced in God's Law against all sinners (Deut. 27, 26). And they that make a sport of sin cannot avoid God's curse, no more than they that feasted when they should have fasted, " 'Surely this iniquity shall not be purged from you, till ye die,' saith the Lord of Hosts." (Isa. 22:14).

The third reason is taken from the stage players, and from such their vices as properly belong to them, as they are stage players. And four of their vices may persuade all men that their plays are unlawful.

First, they, being men, change their apparel, and put on woman's apparel, without which exchange they cannot act some parts in their plays, which thing the Lord forbiddeth. "The woman shall not wear that which pertaineth to the man, neither shall a man put on woman's raiment: for all that do so are an abomination to the Lord thy God" (Deut. 22:5). For this change of apparel makes the man effeminate, and the woman mannish, as some can testify if they would, some have confessed, and the heathen know. Cyprianus,[40] speaking of this change of apparel in stage plays, saith thus: "men lose their manhood" etc. Charondas[41] made a law to the inhabitants of Thuria (which is a city in Greece), described by Pausanias in *Messenicis,* and by Strabo[42] that if any man refused to go to wars, or being in the field cast down his weapons and ran away, he should stand three days in the open market in woman's apparel, which argued effeminateness in him, as if formerly he had used it.

Secondly, they never come on the stage in their own name, but some in the name and person of a devil, others of a fool, others of a bawd, others of a tyrant, others of other men, which beseemeth not a Christian, neither proceedeth it of God, nor is approved of God, but is contrary to Christian profession.

---

40. Bishop of Carthage, and Church Father, 200–258.
41. Sicilian lawgiver, sixth century B.C.
42. Greek geographer, c. 58–25 B.C.

Thirdly, they swear by the living God, which is contrary to the Law of God (Exod. 20:7) or by heathen idols, which is forbidden (Exod. 23:13), or by both, which is reproved (Amos 8:14; Zeph. 1:5).

Fourthly, they teach their hearers and beholders much sin in the acting of their plays, as to swear, curse, lie, flatter, cozen, steal, to play the bawd and the harlot, with very many such other lewd lessons.

The fourth reason arises from the consideration of the hearers and beholders, who being baptized into the name of Christ, are brought into danger of God's wrath, and their own condemnation, inasmuch as they are partakers of the sins of the players and of the plays in approving them. And whatsoever brings men into these dangers must needs be evil. And besides the approbations, which makes them guilty, they learn sin: for as saith Cyprianus, they learn to commit adultery when they hear and behold such immodest and unchaste words and gestures upon the stage. And many go honest thither, which return home dishonest. Job made a covenant with his eyes, that he would not look on a maid (Job 31:1). David desired God to turn away his eyes from regarding vanity (Ps. 119:37).

The fifth reason may be taken from consideration of these eight fruits or effects which follow stage plays:

First, the stage players get their living by an ungodly and unlawful trade, never approved by God, and when they shall stand at the bar of God's judgment, they shall be speechless, and cast into utter darkness, where shall be weeping and gnashing of teeth, except they repent and forsake their wicked trade betimes, while the Lord grants space to repentance.

Secondly, the hearers receive much hurt by them, as was noted in the fourth reason, and if it be true which is reported, whoredom is sometimes committed at that place, and at that time.

Thirdly, the better sort of men which are governors of families, receive damage, when some of their families resort to stage plays, for sometimes their goods are stolen to maintain lewdness, sometimes their daughters or maidservants are defiled, or stolen away, and married without their governors' consent or privity.

Fourthly, the word of God and the ministers thereof, are now and then taxed and taunted.

Fifthly, the Lord himself is there blasphemed ordinarily.

Sixthly, the poor in the Church of Christ are hindered from some relief, which otherwise they might have, for the prodigality lavished upon stage players restrains the liberality that might and ought to be bestowed upon the poor.

Seventh, there is loss of precious time, which should be spent in God's service, by those that are hired to be diligent laborers in his vinyard, and not be wickedly misspent in such sinful sports, seeing everyone, both young and old, must give account to God of his labors, and of his time spent in this life. The Holy Ghost saith: "Redeem the time, for the days are evil; but some men say, 'Let us have pastime,' that is, any sinful course, whereby we may pass away and mis-spend the short time which we have in this life, that the day of death, judgment, and condemnation may come speedily upon us before we repent, and before we consecrate ourselves wholly to God" (Eph. 5:16). Peter saith: "It is sufficient for us, that we have spent the time past of this life, after the lusts of the Gentiles, walking in wantonness, lusts, drunkenness, in gluttony, drinking, and abominable idolatries" (1 Pet. 4:3). And if any be otherwise minded, the Lord in his time will either convert or confound him.

Eighthly, whereas the life of a Christian, effectually called, should be spent continually in fighting against all kind of sin, in crucifying the old man, and in renewing the inner man daily, these stage plays quench the spirit, and destroy the new man, as also on the other part, they foster, cherish, and maintain the old man, as all those that have the spirit of Christ know and feel. But if any man have not the spirit of Christ, the same is not his (Rom. 2:9).

The sixth reason may be taken from the opinion and judgment of all sorts and states of men, by whom these stage plays have been disallowed.

First, all orthodox Protestants of all ages and times, which maintained the general doctrine of the Catholic Church[43] have censured stage plays, as unlawful from age to age hitherto. To report and repeat their several judgments out of their own writings, or out of histories, is more than I can perform, it would make a great volume, it would be tedious to read, and perhaps not so necessary.

Wherefore it seems rather convenient to call a great number of them together out of all the places of their dwellings, and as it were out of all the world, that they all may be heard to speak altogether with one consent and voice. But because it would be a very tedious and troublesome thing for so many, so reverend, and so old, aged Fathers to travel so far, it is more convenient and reasonable to spare their labors so much as may be, and call them together at three several times, and in three several places of their habitations: that is, to call those of Africa, in Africa, those of Asia, in Asia, and those of Europe, in Europe.

In Asia, about two and twenty of the most reverend Fathers of those times, met together in Laodicea, somewhat more than three hundred years after Christ, and holding a council there, decreed that none of the clergy should be present at stage plays.

---

43. I.e., the true believers, even those who lived before the Reformation.

And the Centuriators of Magdeburg[44] have inserted this whole
Council in their laborious and worthy history.

In Africa more than four hundred years after Christ there were
some four and forty of the worthiest and learnedest Fathers assembled at Carthage in the third council that was held there,
among whom was that worthy Augustinus, and they decreed that
the children of ministers[45] or of others of the clergy should not
be present at stage plays, seeing none of the laity might be there,
for all Christians have evermore been forbidden to come in place,
where blasphemers are. And the same religious Fathers then and
there decreed also that the Church should not refuse to receive
the stage players into their fellowship, if they repented and renounced that their trade of playing. Whereby is evident that
stage players in those former and purer times, were generally
excommunicated and cast out of the society of the saints.

In Europe divers worthy and grave Fathers of the Church,
called and summoned by Constantinus Magnus, a little after the
Nicene Council,[46] to come together at Arles in France, held two
councils there, the first, and shortly after, the second. In both
which they decreed the excommunication of all stage players, so
long as they continued that trade of life. And in the first council,
thus they say "as touching stage players, we think it good, that
while they continue in that trade of life, they be kept from the
communion." And in the second council held there presently
after, they decree the same thing again, and almost in the same
words.

But yet to give in more evidence, we may have all the worthy
Fathers of the Churches in Asia, Africa, and Europe, assembled

44. Sixteenth-century Protestant divines who compiled a Church history in
thirteen volumes, each volume embracing a century.
45. Clerical celibacy was widespread from the third century but by no means
universal until the twelfth century.
46. Actually a little before: the council at Arles took place in 314, the Nicene
Council in 325.

together in the sixth general council, which was held at Constantinople, approve that which at Laodicea in Asia, and at Carthage in Africa, was decreed against stage plyers. For when Constantinus Pogonatus[47] in the year 681 called that sixth general council at Constantinople against the Monothelites[48] of those times, as Zonoras[49] sheweth, about five years after, his son Justinianus II assembled the Fathers there again, as Gratianus[50] and the Centuriators of Magdeburg, do witness: and they approved those two former Councils of Laodicea and of Carthage.

And thus we have the judgment of all the orthodoxal and true Catholic Fathers of the Churches throughout the whole world, against stage players, and stage playing, with one consent.

Secondly, the Papists, though they be favorers of stage plays, and actors sometime upon the stage (as lately at Lyons in France), yet they cannot for very shame justify them, but contrarywise condemn them in their writings. And in their great Canon Book of Decrees compiled by Gratianus, they ratify the four first general councils, and all the other councils made afterwards, and contained in that great book of decrees, they approve by name the three councils alleged before. More particularly they approve that which was mentioned before of the Council of Laodicea, and that which was decreed against stage plays in the third Council of Carthage, and the canons of the sixth general council themselves by as in the fourteenth year of Queen Elizabeth.[51]

Fourthly, the civil law in pointing out those persons which are of evil note or name, saith thus of stage players as Pegasus[52] and Nerva[53] said, that those were infamous who tried mastery for

47. Roman emperor from 668–85.
48. Adherents of the doctrine that Christ had one will though two natures.
49. Early twelfth-century Byzantine historian.
50. Twelfth-century Italian founder of canon law.
51. 1572.
52. First-century Roman legal expert.
53. Roman emperor, A.D. 96–98

gain, and all that came upon the stage for a reward. Also who list, may read somewhat to the same purpose.

Fifthly, the infidel heathens, howsoever they first devised them, and after used them very much, yet have they disallowed them, as Augustine rehearsing the words of Scipio out of Tullie,[54] sheweth: "The Romans accounting those plays, and the whole stage to be reproachful, when they valued the goods and enrolled the names of their citizens, gave not the honor of other citizens to stage players but razed their names out of their wards or companies." Suetonius[55] taxeth Nero for a favorer of them, and an actor among them. . . . Arnobius, appealing to the conscience of the heathen, shows that they disallow them, and saith thus of the stage players, "Your own law hath adjudged the stage players to be no honest men."

And these judgments of men are sufficient to condemn stage plays as unlawful, and dishonest also, as Cornelius Nepos[56] saith in his preface before the description of the noble emperors.

The seventh and last reason is drawn from the judgments which God hath inflicted upon the players and beholders.

1. Philip, king of Macedonia, and father of Alexander the Great, was slain at a play by Pausanias, as Diodorus Siculus writes.

2. Plinius, speaking of diverse that died suddenly, saith, that one M. Osilius Hilarus, a noble player of comedies, after he had played his part gallantly on the day of his birth, and was vaunting at supper of his day's work, died suddenly at the table.

3. Paulus Orosius writes that in the twelfth year of Tiberius[57] (which was three years before Christ began to preach the Gospel publicly) there were twenty thousand persons slain by the fall of the theater at Fidena in Italy.

54. Marcus Tullius Cicero, Roman orator and politician, 106–43 B.C.
55. Roman biographer, A.D. 69–140.
56. First-century B.C. Latin historian.
57. A.D. 25.

4. About thirteen years after, Gaius Caligula, the emperor, was slain at a play.

5. About 150 years after Christ's nativity, while the plays were kept at Rome with great solemnity, for the space of three days and three nights together, continually and without intermission, a great part of the city was set on fire and consumed. And Philip the emperor was slain at Verona, and his son at Rome, as it is reported by Sextus Aurelius,[58] Pomponius Laetus, and Eutropius.[59]

6. Tertullianus[60] in his book *de Spectaculis,* saith, that a Christian woman going to the plays, was then possessed of a devil, and when other Christians intending to cast the devil out of her, demanded of him how he durst presume to assault one that believed in Christ, the devil answered, that he found her in his own house, and therefore had good right to seize upon her. Also he writes in the same book and place, that another faithful woman going also to behold the plays had either a fearful dream or a vision the next night after, wherein she was checked for going to the plays, was warned of her death, and died within five days after.

7. Aventinus writes that about twelve hundred years after Christ, three hundred men were slain with hail and lightning at Pisonium, a city of Bavaria, in the confines of Italy, while they were there to behold the plays.

8. The same author Aventinus writes also, that when Pope Nicholas V solemnized his rich jubilee, in the year 1450, with stage plays, five hundred and threescore persons, coming to Rome to behold the plays, were partly trodden to death, and partly drowned in the Tiber.

9. At London in the year of Christ 1583, eight persons were slain and more hurt, by the fall of the theater.

---

58. Second-century Stoic philosopher.
59. Fourth-century Latin historian.
60. Carthaginian Church Father and misogynist, c. 160–240.

10. At Lyons in France in the month of August, in the year 1607, while the Jesuits were acting their plays, to the disgrace of true religion and the professors thereof, the Lord from Heaven continuing thunder and lightnings, for the space of two hours together, slew twelve persons presently, and amazed all the rest with great terror and fear.

Finis